DEATH OF A DIVISION

Death of a Division
by
Charles Whiting

It takes 16,000 dead to train a major-general
Marshal Joffre

STEIN AND DAY/*Publishers*/New York

First published in
the United States of America
in 1981

Printed in the
United States of America

STEIN AND DAY/Publishers
Scarborough House
Briarcliff Manor, N.Y. 10510

B. P.

Contents

Maps

Photographs

Acknowledgements

I would like to thank the following people for their assistance with this book:

BELGIUM: M. Fagnoul (St Vith), M. Kessler (Andler), M. Bach (Schoenberg), M. Held (Herresbach).
GERMANY: Herr Trees, Major Hauprich, Herr von der Weiden, Mr Tom Stubbs, Dr Simons and the staff of the *Aachener Volkszeitung*.
USA: Colonels Matthews and Weldon, Mr D. Coffey, Dr Bouck, Mr Prell, Father Cavanaugh, General Bruce Clarke, Mr C. Boykin.
ENGLAND: Mr Pavey (Imperial War Museum).

C. Whiting, St Vith, 1977

Introduction

On a snowy day in the second week of December 1944, a convoy moved through the Belgian village of Schoenberg. It took the steep road heading east to the front. The trucks, filled with young men in new uniforms, passed the big signboard announcing: YOU ARE ENTERING GERMANY. BE ON YOUR GUARD.

The road wound higher and higher through thick, snow-laden firs. Behind them Belgium lay stretched out like a relief map. But their eyes looked only to the front, to Germany, to the country they had come so far to conquer. The trucks finally halted and the NCOs ordered the men out. Stiff with cold after the long journey, the soldiers, each with the Golden Lion shoulder patch on his sleeve, formed up in columns on either side of the road for the two-mile hike to the forward combat positions. Their guide from the division they were relieving asked the colonel if they were ready. The colonel snapped an order.

'All right, you guys,' the NCOs shouted, 'move out!'

The young men began to 'move out'. The 16,000 men of the 106th US Infantry Division, the newest division on any Allied front, were going into the line.

If the young men were apprehensive as they moved into position, at the point where the deepest penetration into Germany had occurred the previous September, they comforted themselves with the knowledge that this was now the 'Ghost Front', to which new troops were sent to be prepared for 'real combat'. Visiting the Ghost Front two months before, the Ninth US Army historian, Robert E. Merriam, described it in almost pastoral terms:

All was peaceful; farmers in the fields along the road were plough-ing their fields for the winter fallow and some were taking in the last of the summer harvest; cattle were grazing lazily. I was green and my guide knew it, so he said suddenly with a dramatic flourish of his hand, 'See that ridge line over there just across the valley?'
I nodded.
'That's it.'
'What?' I naïvely inquired.
'The German line,' he replied.
We were riding along the top of a huge ridge, silhouetted in plain view of an enemy no more than eight hundred yards away, guns of the West Wall supposedly bristling behind every bush and nothing happened.
'Have to be careful at night,' my talkative guide continued. 'Krauts like to sneak over patrols, just to make a social call. . . . But the only shelling we get is when a Jerry goes to the latrine; seems like they have a machine gun and a mortar there, and each one fires a burst—hope they don't get diarrhoea!'

This, then, was the Ghost Front, where the only casualties were those caused by trench foot and VD contacted in the rest centres. Nothing ever happened here. The eighteen-year-olds of the 106th could look forward to a calm—if very cold—Christmas without fear. In 1945 all was uncertain. But the papers back home were al-ready calling this 'The last Christmas of the war in Europe'. The Germans were well nigh beaten.

But the young men were in for a great shock. Before the week was out their division would be destroyed, and out of the 16,000 men who had gone into the forests, only some 4000 would return. The rest would be killed, wounded or captured, victims of the greatest US defeat in Europe in the Second World War.

Naturally, the events of that week were afterwards glossed over, perverted or conveniently forgotten. General Omar Bradley, to whose Twelfth Army Group the 106th Infantry Division belonged and the commander who had taken the 'calculated risk' (as he called it) of leaving the Eifel–Ardennes so thinly defended, wrote long after the event:

> Troy* was entitled to pride in his VIII Corps, for his divisions had rallied nobly in a furious delaying struggle that emphasized the resourcefulness of the American soldier. Though surprised and disorganized, part of the 106th fell back to the crossroads of St Vith. There it was joined by the 7th Armoured Division in the defense of that road junction.

Brave words, but far from the truth when one learns that that same Troy Middleton, shaken and worried by the events in the hills, was telling the 'hero of Bastogne', General McAuliffe, on 18 December, 'Certain of my units, especially the 106th Division, are broken.' And General Bruce Clarke, who led the 7th Armoured Division 'in the defense of that road junction', gained the impression on his arrival there that 'the 106th no longer existed as an effective division'.

Major Don Boyer of the 7th Armoured also remembers it differently. Leading the 7th Armoured's column towards St Vith, he saw the retreat at its height:

> Here would come an empty two and a half ton truck, then another two and a half, but this time with two or three men . . . in the rear, perhaps an engine crane truck or an armoured car, then several artillery prime movers—perhaps one of them towing a gun, command cars with officers up to and including several full Colonels in them, quarter-tons—anything which would get the driver and the few others he might have with him away from the front. It wasn't orderly; it wasn't military; it wasn't a pretty sight. We were seeing American soldiers running away.

Colonel Dupuy, the historian of the 106th Infantry Division, pulled no punches either in his account of the events of that December. He wrote:

> Let's get down to hard facts. Panic, sheer unreasoning panic, flamed that road all day and into the night.† Everyone, it seemed who had any excuse and many who had none, were going west that day—west from Schoenberg and west from St Vith too.

---

* General Troy Middleton, commander of VIII Corps, to which the 106th belonged.
† The day and night of 16 December 1944.

After the war Major Boyer wrote:

> There was one of the biggest tragedies of St Vith, that American soldiers fled, and by fleeing they crowded the roads over which the reinforcements were coming and prevented those reinforcements from arriving in time to launch a counter-attack to save the 422nd and 423rd Infantry Regiments.

In essence, the cold official prose of the Department of the Army's published account of what happened in the Ardennes to the 106th Infantry Division is much closer to the truth than General Bradley's version. It states:

> The number of officers and men taken prisoner on the capitulation of the two regiments of the 106th Division and their attached troops cannot be accurately ascertained. At least seven thousand were lost here and the figure is probably closer to eight or nine thousand. The amount lost in arms and equipment, of course, was very substantial. *The Schnee Eifel battle, therefore, represents, the most serious reverse suffered by American arms during the operations of 1944-45 in the European theatre.**

Indeed, with the exception of Bataan, it was the biggest surrender of American troops since the Civil War nearly a hundred years earlier.

'It is as great a mistake to return to old battlefields,' someone once wrote, 'as it is to revisit the place of your honeymoon or the house where you grew up. For years you have owned them in your memory. When you go back you find the occupants have re-arranged the furniture.'

The charred hull of the Sherman tank, surrounded by its little cluster of makeshift crosses which marked the graves of its crew, is no longer there. The long, shell-pitted road, draped with white ribbons to indicate that the engineers had swept the verges clear of mines, which once took a week to cover, can be walked now in a leisurely ten minutes. The bunker that held up a whole regiment for eight hours until some young men, 'eager for some desperate

* My italics. C. W.

glory', took it in the end at a cost of fifty per cent casualties, is now simply a gentle mound. Time, progress and the green earth itself have drawn an almost impenetrable cloak over those scenes of desperate action where young men fought and died over thirty years ago.

Normally this is so; but not in the woods of the Snow Eifel where the 106th US Infantry Division came to such a shameful end. Those dark forests are still heavy with the 'feel' of the frightened young men who fought and died there. The foxholes and the rotting remains of the 106th Division are everywhere—the gas masks; the hardly recognizable bits of combat boots and webbing equipment; the rusty rifle clips and ammunition boxes; the shell holes near the road along which the 589th Artillery fled; the lonely grave of Lieutenant Wood. The shame of the 106th Division is still palpable in the forest.

Military history is often written as a mere chronology—a series of moves and counter-moves made by omnipotent, impersonal generals sitting in remote headquarters; generals with the same backgrounds and the same training, looking at the same maps of the same terrain, matching their moral strength and their tactical ingenuity against their antagonists a hundred miles away. But war isn't like that. War is a great tragedy, made up of the dramas and tragedies of many humble men, who have not been consulted on the length of the preliminary softening-up bombardment, the proper manner of isolating the battlefield, the appropriate time for throwing in the reserves. In this book I have attempted to examine the drama and the tragedy of one small segment of that great army America sent overseas in the Second World War: the 106th US Infantry Division. Sixteen thousand young men who, between 16 and 22 December 1944, fought, died and surrendered in the Eifel–Ardennes border area of Germany and Belgium. This is their story.

DEATH OF A DIVISION

One:
The Trap Is Set
Friday, 15 December 1944

'There is nothing to report on the Ardennes Front.'
*Major-General Whiteley, Assistant Chief-of-Staff Operations
SHAEF, 15 December 1944*

I: Old man in the snow

The old farmer walked stolidly across the glittering, snow-covered field. Nothing stirred. Even the birds were silent in the skeletal trees. The heavy snowfall of that second week of December had blotted out the ugly scars of the border fighting of the previous September and had made it impossible for anything on wheels to move save the *Amis'** jeeps. It seemed that the lonely frontier area between the farmer's native Belgium and the German border only a few hundred metres away was devoid of life.

Nevertheless, Nikolaus Manderfeld took care. He was now entering the no-man's-land between the *Ami*-held village of Alfst, in which he lived, and the last, abandoned hamlet before the German line, Allmuthen. If a German sniper spotted him his life might well be forfeit. His younger brother, Anton, didn't like him wandering around outside Alfst. The handful of *Amis* in the village might take him for a spy or courier. They were already highly suspicious of the few locals they had allowed to remain behind to tend the land and the cattle when the border villages had been evacuated the previous September. Nikolaus could well end up in the prison at Verviers.

But on this particular Friday afternoon, eight days before Eu-

* Local name given to Americans.

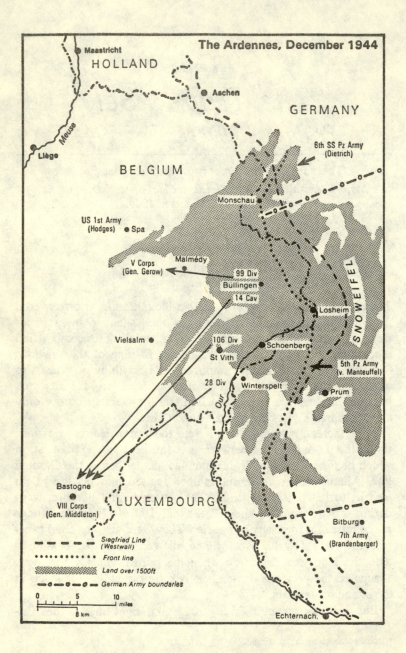

The Ardennes, December 1944

rope's fifth wartime Christmas, he had a special reason for risking his life to visit the old family home at Allmuthen. Not only did he want to check that everything was all right in the empty house, he also wanted a Christmas tree. He plodded on through the knee-deep snow, his leathery face flushed red with the cold, his breath wreathing his head in a grey fog. Suddenly he stopped dead, a hundred metres from the house in which he had been born. There were fresh tracks in the snow! He examined them cautiously. They were not those of deer. The local game had learned to keep away from the front line, although there had been no fighting here for some months now. These tracks had been made by human beings, and to judge by the nail imprints they had been made by German soldiers. The *Amis* normally wore rubber-soled combat boots.

As the old man recalled years later, 'I stood there, wondering to myself whether I should turn back or continue. I took my time and filled my pipe—the bowl could hold exactly two *Ami* cigarettes—and had a careful look round. Nothing. Then the pipe began to have a calming effect on my nerves and in the end I decided to cover the last few metres to our home.'

But the old farmer was not to reach the farmhouse that day nor for many a day to come. Three German soldiers emerged from behind the house, their weapons levelled at him. He had bumped into a patrol. The one in the lead, who had a pair of high-power binoculars strung around his neck, demanded, 'What are you doing here?'

For a minute the old farmer was too shaken and surprised to be able to answer.

'Don't you know that this is a combat area?' the one with the binoculars snapped.

Pulling himself together, Manderfeld explained what he had been intending to do. The hard looks on the Germans' faces relaxed a little and they began to ask him about the American positions in Alfst and Krewinkel, another village a little further west.

Manderfeld, who did not regard his interlocutors as enemy, since most of his early life had been spent as a German national until the Treaty of Versailles in 1919 had made this part of the borderland Belgian, told them what he knew—Alfst was lightly occupied but there were about forty Americans in Krewinkel. The man with the binoculars spoke.

'Tomorrow the heavies'll start firing again,' he declared. 'We'll begin the final offensive. . . . By the day after tomorrow, we'll be in Liège. In four days Antwerp will be ours!'

'The soldiers seemed to think I was very sceptical,' Manderfeld recalled, 'because the one with the field glasses said to me, "We can shoot much better than the *Amis* back there. From up here on the height we can observe all their positions and we're perfect shots. Why, we could shoot that pipe out of your mouth at a distance of three kilometres. Now be off with you, old man, and don't come up here again if you value your life." '

Manderfeld needed no second bidding and hurried back to Alfst as quickly as he could. Panting heavily, he ran into the cobbled yard of the farmhouse in which he lived with the other ten inhabitants of the evacuated village. As he reached the door, he turned to look back, his pipe still in his mouth. There was a sharp crack as a rifle bullet shot off the bowl of his pipe, leaving the stem still clutched between his lips! The German had kept his word.

But that night when the old farmer told his story to the other men clustered around the big stove, his tale of a coming German offensive was greeted with broad smiles. Klaus Manderfeld had always been one for tall stories and no one believed him. There had been no fighting here since September 1944. Why should the Germans pick the week before Christmas, with all the frontier roads blocked or knee-deep in snow, to launch a new offensive, even if they had the men capable of carrying it out, which they hadn't? No, there was nothing to worry about. But at least Manderfeld's strange story had helped to while away another long, boring, cold evening.

In the little houses they occupied, the *Amis* huddled deeper into their khaki-drab blankets. There was no sound outside save the stir of the wind in the firs and the slither of falling snow. The Ghost Front had gone to sleep for another night.

2: We're gonna hang out our washing on the Siegfried Line

At precisely 1805 hours on 11 September 1944, Staff-Sergeant Warner W. Holzinger of the 85th Cavalry Reconnaissance Squadron, 5th US Armoured Division waded across the River Our at Stolzenburg and thus became the first enemy soldier to stand on German territory since the days of Napoleon's *Grande Armée*. All that night and the following days the advancing American First Army swept across the borders of Luxembourg, Belgium and Holland into the Third Reich.

On Tuesday, 12 September, Ernest Hemingway was present as a war correspondent as the 4th Infantry Division crossed the border to be welcomed by 'ugly women and squatty ill-shaped men' who came up to them bearing bottles of schnapps from which they drank themselves to show that the spirit was not poisoned. Hemingway took over a farmhouse, shot the heads off a small flock of chickens and told the farmer's wife to prepare a feast for himself and the staff of Colonel Lanham's 22nd Infantry to which he was attached. That night, as Colonel Lanham recalled, they celebrated the 'happiest night of the war', on German territory:

> The food was excellent, the wine plentiful, the comradeship close and warm. All of us were as heady with the taste of victory as we were with the wine. It was a night to put aside the thought of the great Westwall, against which we would throw ourselves within the next forty-eight hours.

The Allies had reached the celebrated Westwall, or Siegfried Line, on which, as the British Tommies had sung back in 1939, they were 'gonna hang out our washing'. Within three days of the 22nd's first attack on the Westwall, Lanham had lost half his regiment. And he had not been alone. The regiments of the US 1st Infantry Division, the 'Big Red One', and the 30th Infantry Division, 'Roosevelt's Butchers', suffered equally as they tried to force their way through the intricately designed concrete defensive line. Time and again they hurled themselves at the German defences, but without success. In the end, the Supreme Commander, plagued by reinforcement and supply difficulties as well as by the stubbornness of the German defenders, allowed the Ardennes front to settle down into a kind of uneasy co-existence with the enemy, while the attack continued further to the north and south, where there might be a chance of outflanking the enemy. By mid-November, along a sixty-mile stretch of front, facing the Westwall, the war seemed to have come to a standstill.

Beginning in the north at the picturesque frontier town of Monschau in Germany, there is a rugged stretch of thickly wooded, hilly country running southwards for nearly seventy miles until it is cut by the valley of the River Moselle. This range of pine-covered hills, sparsely populated in the main, is called the Eifel, after the Celtic goddess of water, 'Afila'. Basically the Eifel consists of two parallel ridges: the High Eifel (Hocheifel) on the west facing the Belgian frontier and the Volcanic Eifel (Vulkaneifel) on the east, which slopes down to the Rhine. Nearly exactly in the centre of the Eifel there is a 2286-foot-high north–south ridge called the Snow Eifel (Schneeifel) which, together with the continuous river barrier formed by the River Our, effectively bars the way into Germany. Opposite the Snow Eifel, on the other side of the River Our, there is a continuation of the same sort of country into Belgium and Luxembourg, called the Ardennes.

It was into this rough country, with its narrow, winding roads, numerous streams and thick, sometimes impenetrable woods that the Americans made their deepest advance into Germany in September 1944. But, in the end, the Eifel and the Westwall stopped them. Now in November, on the defensive themselves, the Americans relied on the same sort of terrain on the other side of the frontier to stop any German offensive. The High Command reasoned that, although they didn't have a Westwall, they did have the Ardennes.

Not that the Germans would ever attack again. They were beaten. It was only a matter of time before they realized it and gave up. Even the super-cautious Field-Marshal Montgomery had bet Eisenhower, the Supreme Commander, that the war would be over by Christmas.

That winter was the coldest in Europe for a quarter of a century and the 80,000-odd soldiers guarding the Ghost Front were more concerned with keeping warm, getting enough to eat and, if they were very lucky, finding a girl, than in fighting the war.

In the Ardennes, the green division, brought up for combat experience on a 'cold' front before being sent to a 'hot' one, and the veterans, brought out for a rest, found there were luxuries like real beds, hot showers and USO shows. With a bit of luck, they might also get a 72-hour pass, which would take them to Brussels or Liège, where every house around the dingy railway stations was a brothel and where the 'tired but happy' GIs lined up at the Green Cross stations after sexual intercourse to obtain their anti-VD treatment and to have their serial numbers entered in a ledger; without that record they risked a court martial on a charge of being responsible for a 'self-inflicted wound' if they caught a dose.

The Germans had withdrawn their first-line troops from the Eifel–Ardennes area when they realized that the Americans were not going to continue beating their heads against the Westwall and had replaced them by troops of second-line formations, but the troops facing the Americans on the Ghost Front were, nevertheless, contemptuous of their opponents. The *Amis,* they thought, had many faults as soldiers. They avoided close combat and would not attack unless supported by tanks, heavy artillery and air strikes. They did not like to fight at night, nor off the roads. They did not know how to look after themselves in rainy and snowy weather. German spies had observed the long lines of troops suffering from trench foot, their toes purple, with little bits of cotton wool between them to prevent the flesh from coming away as they lay in make-shift first-aid posts. They were not well-motivated and seemed to hate their 'limey' and 'frog' allies more than their 'kraut' enemies. They kept up a continuous chatter over their radios, which always gave their positions and strengths away to the Germans.

However, the 80,000 Americans in the Eifel–Ardennes area thought they had struck it relatively lucky to have been posted to the Ghost Front—'a combination of nursery and old folks' home', as one of them put it in a letter—where there was little likelihood of their being hurt. Their opponents on the German side of the seventy-mile line thought the same. But, in spite of their contempt for their opponents, the German *Landser*'s* sense of security at being stationed on the Ghost Front was marred by an uneasy feeling that the Eifel–Ardennes was not going to remain a *'ruhige Kugel'*† much longer.

3: The eagle's nest

On 12 December 1944 a special bus, which had twisted and turned deliberately and bewilderingly for the last two hours through the hilly, snowbound Hessian countryside and thoroughly confused its high-ranking passengers as to their whereabouts, drew up outside a well-camouflaged, half-underground, heavily guarded headquarters in what appeared to be the middle of nowhere. In fact, the thirty-odd generals in the bus were now outside the *Adlerhorst* (the Eagle's Nest), now code-named *Amt 500* (Office 500), the last of Hitler's headquarters before he retired to his Berlin Bunker to die. Here, two kilometres from Castle Ziegenberg, the 'Great Captain of All Times' would direct his final attack on the Western Allies, the gigantic surprise counter-offensive through the Ardennes.

The immaculately uniformed generals got out of their bus and eyed the unknown HQ, wondering why they had been summoned to this lonely place. They soon found out. Having surrendered their brief-cases—the Führer was not taking any chances that one might contain a bomb, as had happened five months before when von Stauffenberg had attempted to assassinate him—the poker-faced, heavily armed Waffen SS guards ushered them into the conference room. General Hasso Manteuffel, who would command the Fifth Army's attack through the Eifel–Ardennes, described the meeting between the generals and their Supreme Commander years later:

> On one side of the room were the commanding generals, responsible and experienced soldiers, many of whom had made great names for themselves on past battlefields, experts in their trade, respected by their troops. Facing them was the Supreme Commander of the

* German equivalent to 'Tommy' or 'GI'.
† Literally 'an easy ball', what we would call 'a cushy number'.

Armed Forces, a stooped figure, with a pale and puffy face, hunched in his chair, his hands trembling, his left arm subject to violent twitching which he did his best to conceal, a sick man apparently borne down by his burden of responsibility.

Since 16 September, when German troops had been on the run everywhere in the West and he had surprised his top advisers with the dramatic statement, 'I have made a momentous decision. I am taking the offensive. Here—out of the Ardennes!' Hitler had worked flat out to provide new troops—whole divisions, corps, armies—to launch his attack. Now his plan had reached fruition and he was ready to enlighten his bewildered senior officers.

Flanked by his two top advisers, Keitel and Jodl, Hitler lectured his generals for an hour on Prussia's past, in particular how the 'Great Soldier King' had rescued Prussia when the odds had seemed hopeless. Manteuffel noted how 'his style became more assured', and how 'this partially effaced the initial impression that his appearance had produced, at least for those officers who had not seen him in recent months and did not know him well.' Hitler continued:

In the whole of world history there has never been a coalition which has consisted of such heterogeneous elements with such diametrically opposed objectives as the present hostile coalition against us. Ultra-capitalist states on the one hand, ultra-Marxist states on the other. On the one side a dying world empire, that of Great Britain, and on the other a 'colony', the United States, anxious to take over the inheritance. The United States is determined to take Britain's place in the world. The Soviet Union is anxious to lay hands on the Balkans, the Dardanelles, Persia and the Persian Gulf. Britain is anxious to keep her ill-gotten gains and to make herself strong in the Mediterranean. These states are already at loggerheads and their antagonisms are growing visibly from hour to hour. If Germany can now deal out a few heavy blows, this artificially united front will collapse at any moment with a tremendous thunderclap.

Hitler now explained exactly why he had summoned his generals to this remote headquarters. At 0530 precisely on the morning of Saturday, 16 December 1944, three German armies would attack the American front from Monschau to Echternach. In the north the Sixth SS Panzer Army under Sepp Dietrich would smash through the US line between Monschau and the Losheim Gap and, crossing the River Meuse, would roll on through the flat plain of Belgium and reach the Allies' major supply port, Antwerp, by Wednesday the 19th, thus effectively splitting the American and British armies in two.

In the south General Brandenberger's Seventh Army was to play a defensive role, blocking any American counter-attack against the German flank, while in the centre the Fifth Panzer Army under Manteuffel was to break through and capture the two major road and rail centres in the Ardennes, St Vith and Bastogne. But before Manteuffel could capture either objective he would have to surround and eliminate the Snow Eifel salient, the deepest Allied penetration into the Reich. And in order to do that, he would have to destroy the lone American division holding it—the 106th US Infantry Division. But that problem still lay ahead. Now, Hitler was concluding his briefing:

> This battle is to decide whether we shall live or die. I want my soldiers to fight hard and without pity. The battle must be fought with brutality and all resistance must be broken in a wave of terror. In this most serious hour of the Fatherland, I expect every one of my soldiers to be courageous and even more courageous. The enemy must be beaten—*now or never!*

4: The Golden Lions

On the morning of 10 December 1944, the open trucks bearing the 106th Infantry Division began to crawl up the snowy hills in first gear, heading for their new positions in the Belgian Ardennes and, further on, the German Snow Eifel. The young soldiers had had a long and miserable journey. The 106th—or the 'Golden Lions' as they called themselves from their yellow-gold divisional patch—had sailed from the States for England on 20 October. In England it had been planned that they should land at Le Havre on 2 December, from where they would be sent east to take over from the veteran 2nd Division. That would give them three weeks to complete their combat training, so that by early January 1945 they would be in a position to support the expected Allied push in the Ruhr.

But the weather in the English Channel had been so bad that they could not land and had been forced to spend four sea-sick days on board. When they were finally able to land there were no trucks waiting for them and they had waited in the rain and mud of the staging camp at Limesey for another day and night. At last the trucks arrived—but they were open ones, used for transporting supplies, not men. Another two days passed in soaked, numbed misery as the long convoys crawled across Northern France into Luxembourg and from there into Belgium, their new 'home'.

But their troubles were not yet over. They had to wait another thirty-six hours in the cold and wet while the transfer with the 2nd Division took place and they could finally take over the positions now being abandoned by the experienced 'Tomahawk' Division.

Captain Charles MacDonald, then a twenty-two-year-old company commander with the Second's 23rd Infantry Regiment, later a distinguished military historian himself, was present when the Golden Lions moved into his positions near Heckhusscheid in Germany.

> It had begun to snow when our relief appeared the next afternoon. My men were amazed at the appearance of the men from the incoming unit. They were equipped with the maze of equipment that only replacements fresh from the States would have dared to call their own. And, horror of horrors, they were wearing neckties! Shades of General Patton.*

MacDonald didn't know then that the Golden Lions were soon going to 'go down in history as one of the hardest-hit American units of World War II'. So he and his men laughed and let the rookies get on with it.

The men of the 106th were not cheered by what they saw. Their section of the Ghost Front was a dreary, snow-covered, isolated area of low mountains, shrouded by silent, dripping fir forests, dotted here and there with bullet-pocked villages, inhabited by a handful of sullen, German-speaking peasants.

Colonel Boos, one of the Second's regimental commanders, told his opposite number, Colonel Cavender of the 106th's 423rd Regiment, 'It's been very quiet here; your men will learn the easy

---

* In Patton's Third Army even frontline troops had to wear ties all the time.

way.' MacDonald noted, too, that the Golden Lions' officers were 'overjoyed at the prospect of seeing their first combat in such ideal defensive positions and they showed little fear of the thinly spread lines'. Somewhat happier now, the Golden Lions started to settle in to their new 'homes'. Their accommodation was rough. They were housed in the freezing cold Siegfried Line bunkers or timber-roofed dugouts in the forest, from which the veterans of the 2nd had ripped out the stoves and taken them with them. The food was bad as well. For the first two days their rations consisted of the sickly chocolate concentrate, the D Bar, which they had already learned to call 'Hitler's Secret Weapon'. But at least the front was completely quiet and the only casualties they suffered were from trench foot.

But further back the three regimental commanders of the 106th's infantry regiments were not so sanguine about their positions. Colonel George Descheneaux, commander of the 422nd Infantry, for instance, who had no combat experience, now found himself commanding 3000 men in the army's foremost position within Germany, and he didn't like it. On the 14th, when General Jones, the divisional commander, and his assistant divisional commander, General Perrin—one of the few officers in the 106th who had seen action, albeit in 1918—had visited the colonel's CP in the little village of Schlausenbach, Descheneaux had aired his worries. He had only two decent roads to the rear to withdraw his heavy vehicles. Both those roads ran south to north parallel to the German positions. He also felt that he hadn't enough room in the tight valleys all around him to manoeuvre his infantry. Thus if he were attacked by a German force trying to nip out the eight to nine thousand yards of American salient, Descheneaux believed he would have a 'devil of a job' trying to get his men out before they were trapped.

Colonel Cavender, the commander of the 423rd, a much older officer, who had seen action as a GI in the First World War, also had problems. His regiment held a curving line, with one battalion inside the Westwall to Descheneaux's right. But there was a weak link in his deployment—a gap between his riflemen and the German village of Bleialf, where the road ran west into Belgium. If the enemy ever managed to capture Bleialf and push westwards down that minor road, his contact with Descheneaux's 422nd would be severed.

To Cavender's right Colonel Reid of the 424th Regiment was equally unenthusiastic about the positions held by his men. They held the longest front of all—six miles—with a gap of one and a half miles between them and the 423rd. The gap was held only lightly by a scratch force of dismounted cavalrymen and a platoon of Cavender's cannon company. A hundred men to hold 4000 yards—it was not very encouraging, for again if the Germans ever attacked, contact between the 424th and the 423rd could be easily broken.

But all three colonels subscribed to Descheneaux's own doctrine, which he had expressed to his worried staff on the 14th, 'There'll be no retreating for the 422nd!' Even in the unlikely event that the Germans attacked and the three regiments were forced from the key roads and separated from each other, the 422nd 'would stand and fight where they were'.

5: The man they would never take alive

Major-General Alan Jones, the commander of the 106th Infantry Division, was a heavy-set officer of fifty-two. During the First World War he had gone straight from the University of Washington into the army, but he was never sent overseas. Like his Supreme Commander, General Eisenhower, he remained in the States, to his ever-lasting regret. However, he liked the army. He stayed in, and in the lean years of the twenties and thirties, when salaries were low, promotion slow and equipment scarce (there was only one civilian limousine available for the whole US Army, that of the commander-in-chief), he worked his way steadily through the ranks. The war speeded promotion and by 1943 he was a general and assistant divisional commander of the 90th Motorized Division, which he left to take over the recently activated 106th Infantry Division.

The Golden Lion Division was, like all the wartime, non-regular formations, composed mainly of draftees with a few regular officers and NCOs to give it 'backbone'. The division had been organized and trained on the same conveyer-belt principle as American industry. Jones's new men came from every state in the Union and had neither pride in a divisional tradition, as was the case with the Regular Army formations, nor any local attachment, as was the case with the National Guard outfits. The Golden Lions had to be content with an 'instant, pre-fabricated tradition', which in the final analysis meant they were loyal to their buddies and the immediate NCOs and officers who had trained them. But, one year after Jones had taken over command, even this tenuous sense of identification was badly hurt when 6000 of his best riflemen were weeded out to go to Europe as replacements, or 're-inforcements' as they were calling them now in deference to official policy, to make up the losses being suffered by the combat divisions. In their place Jones received a handful of volunteers for the infantry, new draftees, the first of the eighteen-year-old class and men combed out of the supply and quartermaster services, cooks, clerks and the like.

As the division's historian wrote:*

> It would be a grave injustice to the men of the 106th who did remain and go into battle to say they were but culls. The point is that many men who had developed early, who first had shown an aptitude, who were already of the grade of private first class, or higher, were the men chosen to be removed from the Division before it ever left the States . . . one cannot say that these men were of inferior quality. One *can* say that one doesn't take more than fifty per cent of a trained unit's complement away, fill it with other men and expect the unit to enter battle as a combat team.

On 15 December, in his CP, the former Sankt Josef's school in St Vith, General Jones was worried about his young GIs. Not only had they a difficult section of the front to maintain, but they were already proving just how inexperienced and badly trained they were. In the few days they had been in the line, carelessness on their part had set both a regimental command post and a battalion motor pool afire, revealing their positions to the Germans on the hills beyond. Not only that, seventy men had had to be sent to the rear with trench foot, a sure sign that the men didn't know how to

---

* Colonel Dupuy, *Lion in the Way*, Infantry Journal Press, 1949.

look after themselves or that they were encouraging self-inflicted wounds to get out of the line.

The general was also worried about himself. With 16,000 men's lives in his hands, how would he react in an emergency? In all his long army career, he had never yet fired a shot in anger. What would he do if the Germans ever came out of the snow-capped hills to the front of his CP? It was obvious to those around him that he was nervous. At this day's conference at his CP the representatives of VIII Corps, to which the 106th belonged, had pooh-poohed his comment that it was strange the Germans hadn't fired on the targets revealed by the two fires. They told him that the two German divisions opposite his positions, the 18th and 26th People's Grenadier Divisions, were as inexperienced as the Golden Lions and had also been sent there for active combat training.

When Jones told his corps commander, the experienced General Troy Middleton, that there had been 'heavy armoured movement' on his front, the corps staff officer had tried to reassure him.

'Don't be so jumpy, general. The krauts are just playing phonograph records to scare you newcomers.'

That same day he had visited his son, Alan Jones Jr, a first lieutenant serving on the 423rd's regimental staff. Noticing that his father was armed with a smart .32 pistol, the young Jones had remarked jokingly, 'I could use that, dad.'

Jones had smiled but there was no answering light in his eyes as he answered, 'I really should give it to you. But I might need it myself.'

Colonel Welton of the artillery, attached to Jones's HQ, also noted that Jones always kept a number of hand grenades in the front of his Packard, and just before the CP had turned in for the night on Friday Jones had confided in him in all seriousness, 'Welton, the krauts will never get me alive.'

6: The gap

On the same day that the 106th went into the line, Colonel Mark Devine's 14th Cavalry Group took over the classical invasion route westwards, the Losheim Gap, and thus came under the command of General Jones. Devine, a stickler for spit-and-polish and something of a fire-eater in the old cavalry tradition, but with no combat experience, had less than a thousand men under his command at the front. With them he was supposed to guard the link between the 99th Infantry Division of the US V Corps and its nearest neighbour, four miles away, the 106th Infantry Division of Middleton's VIII Corps. Not only was he expected to defend the one natural gap in the American line, he was also to cover a boundary line between corps, where two GIs might be only a foxhole or two apart from each other, but where their actions might be determined by corps headquarters, fifty miles away from one another. To solve the problem Devine dismounted his cavalry, forming them into fortified 'hedgehogs' at the frontier villages of Alfst, Krewinkel, Roth, Berterath, Marlscheid and Lanzerath, with his own headquarters located to the rear at the bigger village and road centre of Manderfeld. Exactly 900 men strung out over four miles, with one battalion of artillery to support them, right in the spot where three divisions, the 3rd Parachute, the 1st SS Armoured of Sepp Dietrich's Sixth SS Panzer Army and the 18th People's Grenadier Division of Manteuffel's Fifth Panzer Army, would launch their great surprise counter-offensive, which would change the history of the world. One thousand against a combined weight of 40,000!

While the 3rd Parachute Division would attack the villages to the north of the gap to force open the way for Colonel Peiper's leading armoured battle group of the 1st SS Panzer, Manteuffel's 18th *Volksgrenadier* would assault those to the south.

Two nights after General Hoffmann-Schoenborn, the commander of the 18th *Volksgrenadier,* had returned from the conference at the Führer's secret HQ, one of his patrols had discovered a gap nearly two miles wide in Colonel Devine's defences which was no longer covered by patrols, at least at night. It was the chance that General Hoffmann-Schoenborn, whose task it was to destroy the 106th, had been waiting for.

On the 15th he discussed it with his corps commander, General Lucht, a very experienced soldier, and the corps commander agreed that it would be ideally suited for swinging round Colonel Descheneaux's left flank. Accordingly the *Schwerpunkt* of the 18th's attack, composed of two regiments, supported by forty self-propelled guns, would go in there, while the 18th's remaining regiment would attempt to capture Bleialf and drive a wedge on Descheneaux's right flank between him and Cavender's 423rd Regiment. Taking a calculated risk, Hoffmann-Schoenborn would leave only a hundred men in the line facing the 422nd to make them believe the German front was still manned. Hoffmann-Schoenborn would personally lead the attack through the Gap.

'*Einverstanden,*'* Lucht said, as they clinked glasses in a toast to the success of the operation. '*Hals und Beinbruch, mein Lieber.*'†

The trap had been set.

In Bleialf the lights went out in the *Gasthaus* hall being used for the USO movie show. At the other end of the attack zone, at Alfst, Farmer Manderfeld slept the 'sleep of the just' in spite of his shock that afternoon.

Further back, to north and south of the Gap, 1st Lieutenant Lyle Bouck of the 99th Division's Intelligence and Recce Platoon at Lanzerath, the link up with the 14th Cavalry, and Sergeant John Bannister, of Lieutenant Farren's platoon of cavalry at Krewinkel, were awake. Both heard alarming noises the previous night. But when they had peered out into the gloom, they had seen nothing. Now, as they rose from their bunks to stare at the stark black hills to the east, they still saw nothing. They did not see 3rd Division paratroopers, in their white camouflage suits, stealing into their positions, nor General Hoffmann-Schoenborn's young grenadiers coming out of the hills, nor the gunners behind them who were making their final adjustments to the 2000 cannon that would go into action at 0530, nor the 980 tanks and assault guns which would back up the first assault wave. The Ghost Front slept, heedless of the muffled tramp of a quarter of a million young German soldiers going to their positions.

It was nearly dawn on Saturday, 16 December 1944. The actors were in their places. The drama could begin.

---

* Agreed.
† Literally, 'neck and bone-break', roughly, 'happy landings'.

Two:
The Trap Is Sprung
Saturday, 16 December 1944

'There are no bad troops, only bad colonels.'
Napoleon

1: The battle of the fortified hedgehogs

Feldwebel Vinz Kuhlbach, a veteran of Normandy and Monte Cassino, switched on the blacked-out torch attached to his tunic, while the eighty-odd men of the 1st Company, the 9th Parachute Regiment, crowded around him in the freezing darkness. Carefully and with dignity, conscious of his rank, he opened the large sealed envelope which he had just been handed by the company commander. This was the reason for their being there; it had to be treated with due respect. He cleared his throat and began to read:

'Regimental Order Number 54, dated 16 December 1944. The Daily Order of the Supreme Commander West. Soldiers, your hour has come! At this moment strong attack armies have started against the Anglo-Americans. I don't need to tell you any more. You feel it yourselves. We gamble everything. You carry within you the holy obligation to give your all, to perform to the utmost, for our Fatherland and our Führer!

Rundstedt.'

The message was received with stunned silence. So that was why they were crouched here in this Godforsaken spot on the Belgian border at this hour of the morning! The German Army was about to launch a counter-attack.

At exactly 0530 an eruption of flame and smoke crashed into the night sky all along the Ghost Front. For over eighty miles,

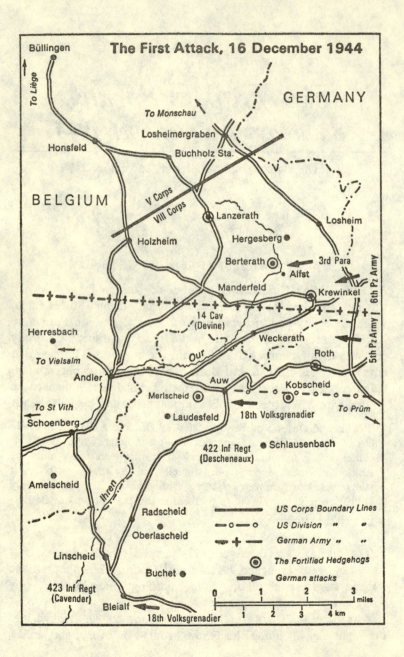

The First Attack, 16 December 1944

some 2000 guns of all calibres and types, ranging from 3-inch mortars to the tremendous 16-inch railway howitzers, roared into action. Behind the men waiting to move off the sky to the east 'was as bright as day'.

In Lanzerath, the paras' objective, Lieutenant Bouck watched, horrified, as 'the whole horizon erupted'. With his platoon he dived to the bottom of his foxhole as the hail of fire swamped the American front-line position. To his rear, at a 99th CP, a staff officer who had been told by Intelligence that the Germans had only two horse-drawn pieces in that sector, cried, 'Christ, they sure are working those two poor horses to death!'

In St Vith, as the first 16-inch salvoes from nearby Prüm began to hit the town, the scared, half-dressed civilians, grabbing their children and most precious possessions, fled for their cellars. Outside in the freezing air, frantic drivers tried to start their vehicles. The jeeps and trucks coughed, spluttered and wheezed like ancient asthmatics. A jeep bounced down the cobbled slippery Hauptstrasse, heading for the Klosterschule, General Jones's HQ. But already the staff officers were running to their posts, as the messages came flooding in: *'0550—from 423rd Infantry* ANTI-TANK CO. SHELLED BY ARTILLERY SINCE 0530 . . . 2nd BN 423rd INF. ALERTED . . . LINES OUT WITH ANTI-TANK CO. 2nd. BN. AND TROOP B 14 CAV. CO.' *'0600—from 28th Infantry Division* DIV. RECEIVING HEAVY SHELLING BY ARTILLERY.' *'0623—from 99th Infantry Division* DIVISION TAKING HEAVY SHELLING ALL ALONG SECTOR.'

Then, almost as abruptly as it had started, the tremendous bombardment ceased. Silence fell on Jones's Ops Centre. The staff officers looked at each other in bewilderment. Behind them the radio and telephone operators relaxed over their suddenly dead instruments. *What the hell was going on at the front?* was the unspoken question in everybody's eyes.

'*Sturm!*' Kuhlbach yelled. The paras forgot the cold and their fear. As the searchlights behind them illuminated the sky to their front with artificial moonlight they doubled forward. Panting heavily in their thick winter clothing, they reached the hamlet of Hergesberg. No opposition. They ran on to the main road to Lan-

---

* The division immediately to the south of the 106th.

zerath. Still no enemy. Suddenly the slow chatter of a heavy machine-gun broke the silence. The paras pushed on. A mortar opened up. Paratrooper Frühbeisser hit the frozen earth at once. Next to him Officer-Cadet Herbert Vogt was a little slower. A fragment of red-hot metal struck him in the throat. He was dead before he reached the ground. The paras had suffered their first casualty and the battle for the fortified hedgehog at Lanzerath had begun.

Up to now Lieutenant Bouck had not been attacked. But ten minutes after the bombardment ceased, the frightened handful of 14th Cavalry holding Lanzerath had bugged out. Now Bouck, a handsome twenty-one-year-old with nearly five years of army service behind him, decided to find out what was going on on the other side of Lanzerath. Cautiously he and his men approached the house which the cavalry had used as an observation post. Its door was swinging to and fro in the wind, indicative of the cavalrymen's hasty flight. But it appeared to be still empty. By means of hand signals, he ordered his men forward. They doubled across the garden and up the stone-flagged path. Bouck rushed through the open door, then stopped dead. A large, heavily built civilian was standing in the room facing the window and speaking over the public phone in German!

The first to react was little Private Tsakainkas, known as Sak, the most aggressive man in the platoon. Pulling out his bayonet, he cried 'Reach!' The civilian might not have understood English, but he understood the gesture well enough. His hands shot up. Bouck did some quick thinking. The man might well be a spy. It looked very much like it. He ought to be executed on the spot. But if the Germans came back and found them, it wouldn't look very good.

'Let him go,' he ordered, indicating the road east with a jerk of his head. Grinning, the civilian fled.

Now Bouck could see through the window what looked like 'hundreds of Germans' coming in their direction.

'Sak,' he commanded, 'you come with me.'

He turned to Robinson, the oldest man in the platoon. 'You and Creger stay here and observe down the road. As soon as that kraut column comes into the home stretch, about a mile down the way, come back up to the platoon.'

Then he ran back to his original position and tried to telephone the 99th. The lines were out. Finally, after a lot of interference by German jamming, he managed to get through, but the officer at the other end would not believe his report of massed German formations.

'Damn it,' Bouck bellowed. 'Don't tell me what I don't see. I've got twenty-twenty vision. Bring down some artillery, all the artillery you can, on the road south of Lanzerath. There's a kraut column coming up from that direction!'

But Bouck waited in vain. No artillery came. Then Robinson's frightened voice came over the field phone, using the wire left behind by the cavalry.

'Lieutenant,' he whispered, 'the krauts are downstairs. What shall I do?'

The Germans hit Krewinkel at dawn in their hundreds and without any covering fire. Nervously the young cavalrymen held their fire. The Germans seemed completely unconcerned. Perhaps they thought the village was abandoned like Lanzerath. No one will ever know, for most of them died that morning. The cavalrymen let them come to within twenty yards of the outer defence wire. Then Lieutenant Farren's troop opened up with everything they had. The Germans stopped as if they had run into a brick wall. Leaving their dead and dying, they broke and ran back the way they had come.

But they soon came again. Once again the Americans beat them off. With fanatical courage, the German infantry attacked again and again. All that morning they attacked, leaving the bleak, wintry fields in front of Krewinkel littered with crumpled bodies. In the end there were 375 of them.

For a while the Germans softened up Troop C's position with heavy mortar fire, using their fearsome six-barrelled, electrically fired mortars. Then they attacked again. All that morning the Germans tried to take Krewinkel. At one point they had captured half the village, but a determined counter-attack by the cavalrymen forced them to withdraw.

Now all the hedgehogs were under attack. Three Platoon of the 14th Cavalry at Roth reported by radio that the Germans were in the village and a tank 75 yards from the platoon command post was 'belting us with direct fire'. Light Honey tanks were dispatched from the 14th Cavalry HQ at Manderfeld to assist Captain Stanley Porche, the officer in charge at the frontier village. They didn't get far. Suddenly 88 mm cannon from nearby Auw opened up. Their 100 lb. shells tore across the valley and the tanks were stopped dead.

At 1100 Captain Porche radioed Lieutenant Herdrich at Kobscheid: 'We are moving back. Your friends to the south are moving back, too [Colonel Descheneaux's 422nd Infantry*]. It's up to you whether you wish to withdraw on foot or in vehicles. I advise you to go on foot.'

That was the last message received from Roth. Shortly afterwards the fortified hedgehog was overrun by General Hoffmann-Schoenborn's triumphant grenadiers. Captain Porche surrendered with ninety men.

At Lanzerath Bouck recognized the men advancing on his positions as paratroopers from their characteristic rimless helmets. There were hundreds of them and he had exactly sixteen men under his command. Admittedly he was in a good defensive position and had automatic weapons. But as they came closer and closer, their arms still slung, he was in an agony of doubt. Should he open fire or should he let them pass? He let the main body pass —300 of them. Then three lone figures came down the road. To Sak, still as eager as ever for action, the three appeared to be the paratroop commander and his aides. He lined them up in the sights of his rifle and prepared to shoot. But at that moment a little girl ran out of a nearby house. He hesitated. If he fired, he might hit the girl. The girl spoke to the soldiers and pointed in the direction of the American positions. The Germans reacted at once. They flung themselves in the ditches on both sides of the road. The battle had begun.†

---

* This statement was incorrect, as we shall see.
† In 1967, Sak, now known as William James, returned to Lanzerath and met Tina Scholzen, the little girl who had given his position away. She is now the mother of three children.

All that morning the 1st and 2nd Battalions of the 9th Parachute Regiment attacked the little village. Sak was in his element at last. Taking over the platoon's .50 calibre machine-gun, he sprayed the woods and ditches, determined that no help should come to the paratroopers trapped on the road below. Meanwhile, Bouck tried desperately to raise the 99th. Finally, he received an answer and called for artillery support. But still none came. With the paratroopers pushing ever closer, he called again.

'What shall we do?' he demanded.

'Hold on at all costs,' came the reply.

A moment later a German bullet hit the radio and he lost contact with his HQ for good. The last remaining link between the 106th and 99th Infantry Division was broken.

At eleven o'clock Colonel Devine, the CO of the 14th Cavalry, returned to his CP at Manderfeld after a quick tour of his forward positions. He found it in a state of panic. His staff were throwing their gear into the waiting vehicles, their engines already running, while the HQ clerks were burning secret papers. Contact had been lost with the 99th Division and there was still no sign of the group's reserve force ordered up to the front. The 32nd Cavalry Squadron seemed to have disappeared.

Devine tried to restore some sort of order. He called Jones at St Vith and asked for an infantry attack 'to save us'. Jones, more concerned with the fate of his own regiments, replied that he could give no infantry support 'at this time'. So Devine said that if he received no aid he would be forced to withdraw to a new defensive line on the Manderfeld ridge. Jones made no comment. Devine added that he would make a counter-attack as soon as his reserve squadron arrived and try to restore his positions at Krewinkel-Roth-Kobscheid. But Jones did not respond to this highly optimistic suggestion. So Devine was left to face up to the problem of the Gap alone.

Now all the fortified hedgehogs had been or were about to be taken. Everywhere the panic-stricken survivors were 'bugging out', as they called it. Troop C, the defenders of Krewinkel, arrived in Manderfeld just as the 32nd Squadron, the reserve, came in from the west. As the two columns passed, the men of the reserve jeered the defenders of Krewinkel, believing they had fled without firing a shot. Following Lieutenant Farren, the men of Troop C went to a hill facing the direction from which the Germans would come and began to dig in sullen, embarrassed silence.

Now the Germans started to slip round the flanks of the 14th Cavalry Group at Manderfeld. Suddenly the reserve squadron bumped into the enemy. A fierce fight broke out. Shells started to fall on the village itself, adding to growing confusion and panic.

Colonel Dugan, Devine's executive officer, called Jones in St Vith. 'The Germans are passing south-west,' he reported. 'They're moving toward the Our.' He then requested permission to withdraw the 14th Cavalry to a line of ridges between Holzheim and Andler, covered by a small tributary of the River Our. This time Jones gave his permission.

The cavalrymen scrambled to get out of Manderfeld before the Germans came. In their haste they set fire to the whole village, trying to destroy the last of their secret documents. It was a case of *sauve qui peut*. The roads west were clogged with vehicles fighting their way through disheartened and demoralized soldiers on foot. Trucks skidded off the slippery roads into ditches. Vehicles which ran out of fuel were abandoned. Platoon leaders told their men to throw away heavy equipment so that they could move faster. The broken cavalrymen needed no such orders. Soon it would be their rifles. Now the Gap was wide open and the Germans began to pour in.

2: The attack on the Snow Eifel

Colonel Cavender's 423rd Regiment at Bleialf was hit first. The assault troops of the 18th *Volksgrenadier* Division advanced immediately their initial mortar barrage had ceased. Cavender knew the importance of the village. If the enemy could break through the single anti-tank company which held it and continue down the road to Schoenberg, he would be cut off from Descheneaux's 422nd. He ordered Colonel Nagle to contact Jones and ask for the release of his 2nd Battalion, the regimental reserve. Curtly Jones refused. Cavender would have to make do with what men he already had. Jones was not going to throw in his reserves at this stage of the battle.

Cavender ordered a scratch force up to help the hard-pressed anti-tank crews, but by the time they arrived, they found half the village already in German hands. Immediately they counter-attacked. A bitter fight ensued around the church. Two days later when the priest emerged from his cellar, he found over 200 dead bodies, both German and American, in the area. Snipers were ejected by bazooka men, who risked their lives in the cobbled streets to stand in the open and blast all of the houses in which the snipers were hidden.

The village changed hands again, and once again the Germans counter-attacked and recaptured it. The weary infantry of the 423rd went in once more and finally, as the sky began to darken, Bleialf was American again. But as they flopped down exhausted in their re-won positions and the German attacks died away, they little realized that the cavalry two miles to their south-west were already beginning to withdraw. Bleialf was held, but thanks to the withdrawal of the 18th Cavalry Squadron, Cavender's flank was in the air.

Colonel Descheneaux's 422nd Regiment was hit last. At first General Hoffmann-Schoenborn had not envisaged a frontal attack on the 422nd's positions around Schlausenbach. Indeed that dawn Descheneaux's 3000-odd men were faced by exactly 100 *Volks-grenadiers*. By noon, however, the first of the Germans began to penetrate through the wide-open gap towards the 422nd's rear. Descheneaux acted immediately. He ordered a small task force of two companies to counter-attack towards the hill village of Auw from where the Germans were coming.

The 300 GIs pushed off in good order but almost immediately they were hit by a blizzard. The young Golden Lions struggled on through the bitter, flying snow, forcing their way up and down the steep forest trails. At two in the afternoon they emerged from the woods and were ready to launch their attack on the little group of white-painted houses clustered around the church on the hill to the front. Then the enemy spotted them and heavy fighting broke out as the GIs stumbled towards the village. But as they reached its outskirts an urgent radio message came through from Descheneaux. German infantry were coming through the woods towards the CP from the east and the little task force was urgently needed back at Schlausenbach. So the men did an about-turn and started back the way they had come.

Behind them on the other side of the road that led from Auw, Major Arthur Parker III, the acting commander of the 589th Artillery, realized that he was in danger of being cut off from the 422nd, the regiment his battalion supported. He decided to send some of his gunners out as local protection. One group, under Lieutenant Leach, got within 300 yards of Auw when the Germans opened fire and the group was pinned down. Undaunted, Leach called down his own fire to cover him. As the 105 mm howitzer shells thudded into Auw, Leach and his men sprang to their feet and pelted through the snow to safety.

Now, alerted to the Americans' presence, General Hoffmann-Schoenborn, who was commanding the right thrust of the 18th *Volksgrenadier* Division in person, sent in assault guns to root the enemy out. Lieutenant Eric Wood, Battery A's executive officer, rushed to a small hill on the battery's left flank from where he could see the assault guns more clearly. Like primeval monsters they crawled towards the American positions, guns hanging long and low.

Wood did not hesitate. 'Number four gun,' he bellowed, 'Fire!' The first shot struck home. The tank stopped dead and began to burn fiercely.

Another German assault gun took up the challenge. The American gunners, using the smallest possible fuse, aimed and fired again. There was the hollow booming sound of metal striking metal.

Now other howitzers of Arthur Parker's battalion joined in the battle. Expertly, the six-man crew of each gun slapped in bags of explosive, placed the shells on their trays, thrust them into the breech and rammed them home. Other gunners armed with bazookas went tank-hunting, creeping as close as they dared to the assault guns and firing their rockets.

Hoffmann-Schoenborn sent in his infantry, but Wood reacted quickly to the new challenge. He snapped a quick order to the crew of number four gun and they changed their ammunition from armour-piercing to shrapnel. Using short-time fuses, the gunners swept the area with shells. Bursting in the air, the red-hot, fist-sized fragments scythed down the grenadiers. They began to run back the way they had come, leaving the snow littered with corpses.

But Hoffmann-Schoenborn was not prepared to give up. He ordered his 'screaming meemies' into action. With a stomach-churning howl the salvo of six shells hissed into the sky.

'Hit the dirt!' Wood yelled.

The gunners needed no urging. Next moment the barrage swamped them in a murderous wave of steel. Within the hour, thirty-six men of A Battery would be dead.

While the inexperienced commander of the 422nd Infantry Regiment, who was still not unduly worried about his position around Schlausenbach, swung his left battalion round to face north ready to link up with the relief force he anticipated soon from St Vith, his neighbour Colonel Cavender radioed General Jones: 'We'll hold our present positions until ordered differently.'

As dusk fell the fighting in the Snow Eifel began to die away. On both sides the infantry dug in. General Hoffmann-Schoenborn was well content with the efforts of his young grenadiers that day. They had taken all their objectives save Bleialf, and they deserved a rest.

Cavender and Descheneaux were also quite pleased with themselves. They had suffered few casualties and had held most of their positions. Admittedly Descheneaux knew he had lost contact with his neighbours, the 14th Cavalry, just as Cavender had lost all but radio contact with Descheneaux. In a way they were cut off. But the fact did not seem to worry them. Both were content to settle into their CPs for the night. At the CP of Cavender's 3rd Battalion the officers crouching around the wireless in the hissing glare of the Coleman lamp heard the BBC announcer say, 'The German offensive has reached the Belgian border in three places.'

'Well,' someone commented, 'the folks back home seem to know more about it than we do.'

So they sat and waited, having decided to do nothing until

morning. It was a fatal decision for the 8000 Golden Lions now left on the wooded heights of the Snow Eifel.

3: St Vith

The town of St Vith was in the grip of panic. The bombardment from nearby Prüm had been going all day and in the Luxemburg-strasse and Prümerstrasse which flanked General Jones's HQ there were already smoking ruins where once there had been solid houses. By the time the attack was over, there were only three houses left standing in the whole town. Most of the inhabitants were huddled in the cellars. Many had first found refuge in the great cellar under the 106th's HQ, but as the day progressed and the Americans became more and more frightened, they were turned out to find shelter elsewhere. The Americans' attitude towards the local citizens had changed, too. Whereas they had been quite friendly the previous day, now they were cold and withdrawn.

A staff group under Captain Keller of the 106th was quartered in Frau Margret Doepgen-Beretz's house in the Klosterstrasse. Up to the day of the attack Captain Keller and his men had been very friendly to the Belgian family, but this Saturday they did not hand the civilians their daily rations.* Instead they turned their backs on them. Captain Keller began to roll up the charts on the wall of what had once been Frau Doepgen-Beretz's sitting room.

'Are you going away?' she asked in English, but she got no answer.

By now the first of the stragglers, dirty and demoralized, were beginning to make their way along the main street, ankle-deep in mud and littered with debris. Private William MacDonald, a jeep driver with the 740th Field Artillery, who had been attached to the 2nd Division before the 106th had taken over, eyed them with disdain. The day before he had nicknamed the green rookies of the 106th 'the Sick and the Hungry'. But there had been no malice intended. Now he was angry with them. They were bugging out

---

* For several months the Belgian Government refused to feed the locals because they regarded them as Germans and traitors.

just because they were taking a little artillery fire. It was too much for him. Without hesitation, he pushed his way through the crowd of soldiers and roared at the officer, 'Why, you're a goddam coward!'

The colonel did not even seem to hear him.

That evening, as General Jones waited for some word from his corps commander, he knew that all his three regiments in the line had been under attack, but he didn't yet know just how serious the situation was. He had still to learn of the 14th Cavalry's débâcle in the Gap.

In his command post officers stood around in little groups, whispering in grave tones. The clerks and radiomen glanced up nervously every time the door opened, as if they expected the Germans to come bursting in at any moment. But it was Brigadier-General William Hoge, commander of the 9th Armoured Division's Combat Command B, who strode into the CP, sent by General Middleton.

'You've heard about it?' General Jones asked quickly.

'I haven't heard anything,' Hoge answered in his abrupt manner which had made him many enemies in the army and delayed his promotion. 'I was reconnoitring up in Monschau. General Gerow* told me my outfit was released and I was to report to you. I came straight on down.'

'It's bad,' Jones exclaimed, not realizing how much Hoge hated any kind of emotionalism. 'They've hit my whole front around the Eifel. Two regiments are nearly cut off.'

'What shall I do?' Hoge asked.

'Move your combat command up here right away. I want you to attack toward Schoenberg tomorrow morning. Bring my regiments back!'

General Hoge stamped out of Jones's office without comment. The situation at the 106th CP was definitely bad, he thought. He then set about trying to find a phone so that he could contact his command. While doing this, he bumped into Colonel Devine.

'What the devil's happening out there, colonel?' Hoge asked.

* Head of V Corps, to which the 9th's CCB had been attached.

Mumbling an incoherent answer, the colonel brushed past Hoge and went into Jones's office where the general and Colonel Slayton were waiting for him. Slayton had been assigned to the 106th by Middleton 'to help get the division on its feet' and counteract the pessimism of the 106th's G-2, who was thought at corps to be a 'nervous nelly', who spent his time fretting about petty problems.

Jones was obviously shocked by Devine's state, but because of his own combat inexperience and concern about the fate of his two regiments in the Snow Eifel, he did not see that, as Slayton put it, 'the man was completely demoralized by events' and had 'little knowledge of the location of his troops'. After dressing Devine down, instead of relieving him as Slayton believed Jones should have done, he sent him back to his unit, which, unknown to any of those present, was already retreating again, leaving the way wide open for the complete encirclement of the regiments in the Snow Eifel.

Before Slayton could protest, an aide popped his head round the door and said, 'Excuse, general, it's the corps commander on the phone.'

The conversation between Jones and General Middleton was to play a decisive role in the fate of the two regiments. Because both men suspected that the excellent German radio listening service might be eavesdropping, their language was very guarded and sometimes ambiguous, with unfortunate consequences for the two trapped regiments.*

'I'm worried about some of my people,' Jones began, shouting because the connection was bad.

'I know.' The corps commander guessed Jones was referring to his regiments in the Snow Eifel. 'How are they?'

'Not well. And very lonely.'

'I'm sending up a big friend,' Middleton reassured Jones. 'Workshop. It should reach you about 0700 tomorrow.'

Jones's heart leapt. 'Workshop' was the code name of the 7th Armoured Division, presently belonging to the Ninth US Army and located at Maastricht on the Dutch–German border.

---

* The late Colonel Peiper, who led the spearhead of the 1st SS Panzer Division, told the author that throughout the battle he knew his opponents' aims, thanks to radio-listening teams.

'Now about my people,' Jones continued, feeling much better. 'Don't you think I should call them out?'

Later, during the inquiry into the conduct of the 106th and the 14th Cavalry during the battle, Middleton said he didn't hear that question due to the bad connection.

'You know how things are up there better than I do,' he said. 'Don't you think your troops should be withdrawn?'

Again luck was against the 106th in this fateful conversation. This time it was Jones who didn't hear the corps commander's question. He insisted, 'I want to know how it looks from where you are. Shall I wait? Is there time?'

But General Jones's questions remained unanswered and when he hung up he was convinced that his corps commander meant him to keep his men in the Snow Eifel. Perhaps he should have argued with Middleton, but being new to the front and with no combat experience, he thought that Middleton might think him overly cautious. So the issue of the two regiments was left in the air. Turning round to Colonel Craig, one of his artillery officers, he said, 'Well, that's it. Middleton says we should leave them in. Get General Hoge.'

Craig went out, telling himself that the two regiments were as good as lost unless a miracle happened. Jones, a little happier now, faced Colonel Slayton. 'But here's some good news. I'm getting the Seventh Armoured. They'll be here early in the morning.'

Slayton was in a quandary. He knew that under the conditions pertaining at the front and at night, it would be impossible for the 7th to cover the ninety miles or so from Maastricht and arrive at St Vith early in the morning. He opened his mouth to protest, then closed it again.

'I should have said so,' he admitted after the war, 'but that would have meant that I should have to have called the corps commander a liar.' And colonels don't call corps commanders liars if they want to stay in the army. So he said nothing.

Hoge re-entered the office. 'The Seventh Armoured is coming,' Jones told him. 'They'll be here tomorrow around seven a.m.'

The general walked over to the big wall map. He pointed to the village of Schoenberg directly behind the two regiments in the hills. Lying in the valley below, it would be the main objective of the 18th *Volksgrenadier* Division the next day, but Jones did not know that.

'I'm going to have the Seventh attack Schoenberg instead of you, Hoge. I want you to take Winterspelt here.'

All along their line Colonel Reid's 424th Regiment had held the attack of the German 62nd *Volksgrenadier* Division, but at the village of Winterspelt a serious situation had developed. Reid had used up all his reserves, and one of his artillery battalions, the 591st, had fired nearly all its ammunition—over 2600 rounds during that day. His position was nearly as serious as that of Descheneaux and Cavender. Now Hoge's tanks had been switched from the north to the south; everything in the north depended on the early arrival of the 7th Armoured.

And in Bastogne, VIII Corps HQ, the corps commander told a staff officer who had just entered his office, 'I just talked to Jones. I told him to pull his regiments off the Schnee Eifel.'

4: The 7th to the rescue

The 7th Armoured Division at Maastricht was alerted on the evening of the 16th to 'help out' in a 'little German counter-attack of three or four divisions'. It was an unfortunate time to alert the division. A third of the men were in high spirits because they were going on leave to Paris and Brussels after three months of combat. Another combat command was preparing for a cavalrylike swoop on the last German outpost west of the River Roer. At headquarters staff officers were explaining the complexities of American baseball to the Dutch. Knowing that the division was going to be in Maastricht for some time, they had organized a baseball league and were amazing the locals with the niceties of this, to them, unknown sport. Thus when the assistant operations officer dashed in to the office to say that the division was alerted for immediate movement, as Captain Robert Merriam said, 'the bombshell burst'.

Immediately the new divisional commander, General Robert Hasbrouck, an experienced armoured commander, began to alert his command, spread out all over that part of Holland, for a night march southwards. They would move in two columns: one to the east and one to the west, and both, unknown to Hasbrouck, in the direct path of the leading panzers of the 1st SS Division under *Obersturmbannführer* Jochen Peiper.

Leading this motorized march southwards would be General Bruce Clarke, the commander of the 7th's Combat Command B. Hasbrouck called Clarke at his headquarters in Eubach, just across the frontier in Germany. The phone call caught Clarke just as he was finishing his packing for a seventy-two-hour leave in Paris. It hadn't been Clarke's idea to take a leave, but he was suffering badly from piles, probably brought on by five months of combat, and Hasbrouck himself had ordered Clarke to go.

Now he said, 'Bruce, I'm afraid you can't go to Paris after all. The division has just got orders to move down to Bastogne.'

'Bastogne!' Clarke exploded. 'That's practically a rest area. What're we going to do down there?'

'I have no idea,' Hasbrouck replied. 'General Simpson* told me to go down and report to Troy Middleton. You go on ahead and find out what the mission is. Maybe they're having a little trouble down there.'

Hurriedly Clarke changed into his combat gear and threw a few things into the battered old Mercedes which Hasbrouck had loaned him. Together with Major Owen Woodruff and two drivers, one of them driving the following jeep, the little expedition set off in the pitch darkness for Bastogne. A few minutes after they had left, Hasbrouck heard from corps that the 7th was needed at Vielsalm, *not* Bastogne. Half an hour later that objective was changed, too. For the first time the harassed staff officers, waiting for road clearances and feverishly working out the details of the march south, learned that their real objective was St Vith. But by then General Clarke had long since vanished into the night.

There was a great difference in the personalities of the two generals who would decide the fate of the 106th Infantry Division the following morning. Jones was a typical infantryman, cautious and plodding. In addition, he had had no combat experience in the

* Commander of the Ninth US Army.

whole of his career. It is often said that a professional soldier trains all his career for something that nobody wants to happen. Jones had trained all his life for that eventuality but, as we shall soon see, when it did happen his training did not help him one bit.

Bruce Clarke, a huge man with a craggy face and wavy hair, was different. An engineer by training, he had first gone into action on 31 July 1944 as the head of Combat Command A in General Patton's favourite armoured division, the 4th. Soon after the 4th had started its lightning drive across France, Patton visited Clarke and asked if he needed any help. Clarke, unabashed in the presence of the army commander, told Patton that he was 'working under superiors who were accustomed to a two miles an hour advance and I often ran out of orders by 1030 in the morning. What am I supposed to do in such cases?'

Patton's answer was typical. 'Go east, Clarke,' he said.

Thereafter Clarke went several hundred miles, but his advances did not endear him to his superiors and Patton himself warned Clarke, 'Don't try to fight the whole war!'

In October, when the Third Army reached eastern France, Patton came to see Clarke and told him, 'Clarke, you are a damned nobody!'

Clarke stared at him in astonishment. Patton then explained that on the previous evening he had had dinner with General George Marshall, the head of the US Army, who was visiting Europe, and had asked him why he didn't promote Colonel Clarke. Marshall asked if Clarke had ever served at Fort Benning. When Patton replied in the negative, Marshall said, 'I don't know him.'

'Hell, Clarke, if you had been an infantryman instead of an engineer and had served at Fort Benning you would be a major-general by now,' said Patton.

But General Marshall must have looked at Clarke's file, for on 1 November he was ordered to transfer to the 7th Armoured Division in Holland where there was a vacancy for a brigadier-general. Clarke was sorry to leave the Third Army, but he was ambitious and wanted promotion.

This, then, was the man now speeding through the night towards the battle. He was experienced, ambitious and a little ruth-less, like all the armoured commanders who had served in Pat-ton's Third Army. Jones would hesitate to order his men into battle if he thought they were going to suffer heavy casualties. Clarke would, too, but if he thought that the resultant success would outweigh the losses incurred, he would give the order with-out hesitation.* In essence, the coming confrontation between the two very dissimilar generals and what followed was to mean that one of them had honours heaped upon him and rose to the highest rank in the US Army, while the other left it in ignominy.

5: Complete success is now within our grasp

Midnight fell on the Ardennes front. At his headquarters in the Eagle's Nest, Hitler called *General der Panzertruppe* Balck, a broad-faced armoured expert at Army Group G HQ, and told him, 'From this day on, Balck, not a foot of ground is to be given up. Today we march!'

Balck listened as the Führer explained how the ISS point under *Obersturmbannführer* Peiper of Dietrich's Sixth SS Panzer Army was well into the Gap and about to break loose, while Man-teuffel's Fifth had about cut off the Snow Eifel with Lucht's corps and was preparing his drive to the River Meuse with his remaining two corps. Hitler ended with an enthusiastic outburst of the kind unknown to Balck for many a month. 'Balck,' he cried, 'every-thing has changed in the West. Success—complete success—is now in our grasp!'

Closer to the front the German commanders were not so san-guine. *Obersturmbannführer* Peiper at that moment had just flung open the door of the Café Palm at Lanzerath to find the place full of officers, mostly asleep, and wounded American prisoners,† with a full colonel dozing at his desk. To Peiper, eager to be on his way, it looked as if the 'front had gone to sleep'. Paratrooper Frühbeisser, who was awake, heard an argument develop between

---

* In the Third Army, commanders had followed Patton's own motto that 'movement means fewer casualties'.
† Among them was Bouck, wounded in the leg, and 'Sak', his cheek shot away, his right eye lying limply in the gaping wound.

the 9th Parachute Regiment commander and the SS officer. Peiper, slim and tough, hardened by the battles in Russia which had gained him the Knight's Cross and the coveted oak leaves, plus the command of the 1st Panzer Regiment at the age of twenty-eight, was contemptuous of the paratroop colonel. He was obviously a 'base stallion' with no combat experience, who had been drafted into the paras from Goering's Air Ministry. Colonel Hoffmann of the 9th Para, on the other hand, thought Peiper was being unrealistic. His regiment had suffered heavy casualties during their first day of combat and he didn't want to risk any more. The SS colonel pooh-poohed Hoffmann's fears about the woods being full of Americans in pillboxes, covered by mines and automatic weapons. He rode rough-shod over Hoffmann, ignoring the fact that the colonel was much older and senior to him in rank. He demanded and got the 1st Parachute Battalion to which Frühbeisser belonged. They would cover his tanks while they made a night attack on the village of Honsfeld.

Peiper strode to the nearby house which had been fixed up as his CP and planned his attack. If it succeeded, it would place him directly in the path of the eastern wing of the 7th Armoured moving down to the rescue of St Vith!

General Lucht, commander of the German 66th Corps, was not too happy, either. His 62nd *Volksgrenadier,* as green and confused as the 106th, had failed to break through Colonel Reid's 424th Regiment at Winterspelt. But Hoffmann-Schoenborn's 18th *Volksgrenadier* had done well against the other two regiments of the 106th. All the time Lucht was fairly confident about the morrow. He had ordered the 62nd *Volksgrenadier* to break through the 424th line at the village of Heckhusscheid and drive for the Our valley 'at all costs'.

Meanwhile Hoffmann-Schoenborn's 18th *Volksgrenadier* would complete his drive through the Gap with his left wing. His right wing would take Bleialf and fight its way down the road to Schoenberg, thus separating the two American regiments. There, at the village of Schoenberg, the two wings of the 18th *Volksgrenadier* would link up, the Americans on the heights would be trapped, and the 18th could get on with the vital attack on St Vith.

Manteuffel had impressed upon him most strongly that he had to have St Vith by the 17th.

Just after midnight an aide brought him the latest forecast for Sunday's weather, prepared with the help of the secret German weather station at Spitzbergen:* 'cloudy to thick' with an increase 'in wind strength and patches of fog in central Belgium'. That meant that Allied air support would be unable to interfere with his operations.

It was 'Führer weather'. Even if the two American regiments soon to be trapped on the heights, who had remained strangely inactive all that day, did decide to counter-attack on the morrow, there would be no help coming to them from the American fighter-bombers.

* Unknown to Allied Intelligence, a group of German scientists and military personnel had established a secret weather station at Spitzbergen, from whence they forecast the weather for Europe. The station was not discovered until three months *after* the war had ended.

Three:
Hell's Highway
Sunday, 17 December 1944

'Until division tells me definitely to move, I'm staying
right here.'

Colonel Descheneaux to Colonel Cavender,
17 December 1944

1: Peiper's tigers

At just after four o'clock on the morning of Sunday, 17 December, a long line of US vehicles was edging its way slowly through the little village of Honsfeld. They were the survivors of the 14th Cavalry Group, fugitives from yesterday's battle, fleeing for their lives or attempting to make what Colonel Devine called the '14th Cavalry's last delaying line'.

A soldier in an unidentifiable uniform waited in the ditch until the last vehicles had passed. Then he clambered on to the road, littered with abandoned equipment, and clicked his darkened torch on and off a couple of times in some sort of signal. For a few moments nothing happened. To the east the night sky flickered a faint pink—an artillery barrage. Then two shapes, outlined faintly by the pink light, came into view. The man with the torch turned and began to walk towards Honsfeld. Behind him the two Shermans followed slowly, their commanders in their turrets, the gunners squatting behind their 75 mm cannon, ready to open up at once. And behind them came *Obersturmbannführer* Peiper and the head of his combat infantry, Diefenthal, riding in a Volkswagen jeep, with Peiper still fuming at having to waste so much time. They drove past some abandoned anti-tank guns and ar-

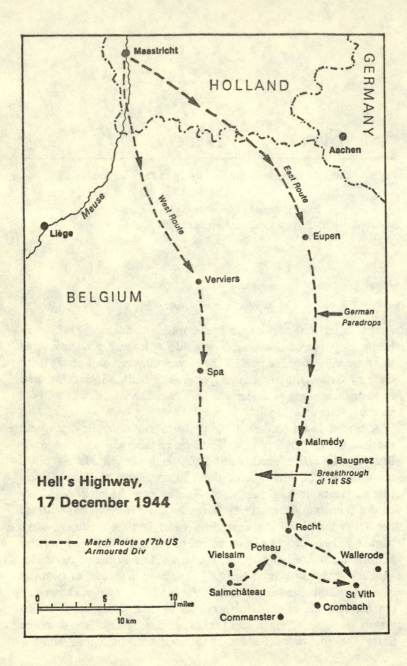

GERMANY

HOLLAND

Maastricht

Aachen

Meuse

West Route

East Route

Liège

Eupen

German
Paradrops

BELGIUM

Verviers

Spa

Malmédy

Baugnez

**Hell's Highway,
17 December 1944**

Breakthrough
of 1st SS

Recht

– – – – – *March Route of 7th US
Armoured Div*

Poteau

Wallerode

Vielsalm

Salmchâteau

St Vith

Crombach

Commanster

0   5   10 miles

10 km

moured cars and Peiper's rage gradually began to evaporate. This was going to be a walk-over.

In one of the little stone houses at the outskirts of the village Lieutenant Reppa of the 14th Cavalry was dozing in a hard up-right chair when he became conscious of a change in the sound of the traffic which had been rumbling by all night. He opened his eyes and said to First Sergeant William Lovelock, 'They don't sound like ours.'

He went to the door and opened it. A long line of armoured ve-hicles was rumbling by, packed with infantry. A tank followed, twice the size of any tank used by the US Army.

'Oh, my God,' he said and closed the door quickly. 'They're Germans!' Angrily he spun round on Lovelock. 'Why didn't Creel warn us?' he demanded.

Just at that moment Sergeant Creel, who was in charge of the roadblock outside the village, came hurrying in through another door.

'I was in my armoured car,' he explained excitedly. 'A guy came walking down the road in front of a big vehicle, swinging a flashlight. Biggest damn tank I've ever seen. With a swastika on it!'

'Why the hell didn't you shoot?' Reppa cried.

'I figured it'd be best to warn everyone. So here I am.'

There was no time for recriminations. If they didn't get out at once, they would be trapped.

'Get the men ready,' Reppa ordered, grabbing his helmet. 'We're moving out of here. It's dark and we'll just pull into their column. When we come to a crossroads we'll turn right and beat it.'

But Lieutenant Reppa's luck had run out. Just at that moment one of Peiper's Tigers came to a halt outside the house. Men of the 1st Para Battalion dropped to the ground, their machine pis-tols at the ready.

'Come on out!' one of them yelled in English.

Reppa hesitated. Upstairs he had a room full of wounded troopers. His shoulders sank in defeat. 'We can't make it. . . . We can't do a damn thing.'

Slowly as if in a trance, he walked to the door and opened it.

There were paratroopers everywhere. Raising his hands, he called the one German word he knew. *'Kamerad!'*

Peiper's Tigers rattled through the village, firing at everything and in all directions, in order 'to create panic and secure the rear exit', as he put it. Half-clad soldiers shot out of the houses, surrendering or trying to escape. A panic-stricken GI blundered into the house of the village priest, Father Signon.

'Father,' he cried, 'the Germans are coming.' He flung a terrified glance over his shoulder. Father Signon showed him a path by which he might escape, just as the paras barged into the house demanding schnapps and food. An SS officer grinned at the middle-aged priest.

'You remember me, father?' he asked. Signon shook his head numbly.

'Well, I'll tell you when you last saw me,' the SS officer said, pleased to have been able to surprise the priest. 'I was here exactly two weeks ago and spoke to you. In American uniform, of course!' He laughed at the look on the village priest's face.

Not all the SS officers were so pleasant. Peter Mueller, who had fled with his family from Manderfeld along with the Americans, was now lined up with the captured 14th Cavalrymen. An SS officer, pistol in hand, eyed the scared civilians.

'I'm going to shoot all you partisans myself,' he announced. *'Grenzpack!'* *

An SS man punched Mueller in the face as he and the others were herded into a big shed at the edge of the village. There were eighty of them in all, American and Belgian. Mueller knew that he and his nephew were now in serious trouble. One of the SS guards whispered to him out of the side of his mouth, 'Tell the officer you didn't fire on our troops. Quick, unless you want to be shot.'

Mueller again told the officer that he hadn't fired on the Germans as they had driven into Honsfeld. But the officer didn't believe him. They were formed into a column and marched off in the direction of Lanzerath. Mueller looked anxiously for some way to escape, but they were too heavily guarded. In Lanzerath they arrived at a barn just opposite the Café Palm, where Bouck and Sak

* Border mob.

still lay wounded. An SS man cried, 'In there, you're going to be shot now!'

Mueller's nephew, Johann Brodel, tried to protest that they were Belgian.* Hardly had he spoken when a pistol cracked and he fell to the ground, a bullet in the back of his head. Horrified, Peter Mueller swung round to attend to him. The pistol cracked again. Mueller screamed as a bullet struck him in the back. A third slug hit him behind the ear. He was swung right round by the impact. Next moment he hit the ground. He was completely conscious but he lay quite still. Satisfied that the traitor was dead, the SS man left the barn. A few minutes later Mueller sneaked out of the barn and fled for his life.

Now, with Peiper through Honsfeld and charging towards Bullingen, where he knew there was an American POL dump and he could refuel, the 14th Cavalry and the men from other units who had attached themselves to the 14th broke completely. Guns and vehicles jammed all the exit roads from the 'final delaying line'. A column of 8-inch howitzers was abandoned. Equipment was dumped. Cooks, clerks, drivers, riflemen, cavalrymen, all inextricably mixed, fled westwards. Village after village was abandoned between Honsfeld and Herresbach. Colonel Devine, his executive officer, Colonel Dugan, his S-3, Major Smith, and his S-2, Major Worthington, took off in a jeep for St Vith, giving no explanation.

'All his eggs in one basket,' Colonel Dupuy, the 106th's historian, wrote somewhat maliciously.

By dawn the whole of the 'final delaying line' had gone. The broken cavalry was streaming right into the path of the 7th Armoured and the road to Schoenberg was virtually wide open.

2: Hell's highway

At the same time that Peiper launched his surprise attack on the 14th Cavalry, General Bruce Clarke arrived at General Middle-

---

* In 1940, when Germany took East Belgium, the three cantons of Malmédy, St Vith and Eupen, which had belonged to her until 1919, were proclaimed German again. Therefore Mueller and the other civilians, suspected of firing on the SS, were regarded as traitors.

ton's HQ in Bastogne. It had been a long, cold drive and Clarke had been forced to hold on to the battered Mercedes' gearstick all the way to keep the car in gear. Middleton's chief-of-staff took Clarke to the corps commander, who was awake although it was four in the morning. He suffered from bursitis and slept badly.

'Hello, Clarke,' he greeted the newcomer. 'You're to go to St Vith and help out General Jones. He's in some trouble out on the Schnee Eifel. Two regiments of the 106th are marooned there.'

'I have just four men with me,' Clarke explained.

'I know. Your division is coming south by two separate routes. Now you go to bed. You can go to St Vith and see Jones in the morning.'

Clarke took the corps commander's advice. If Middleton, who knew the big picture better than he did, was so unconcerned, why should he worry. He left the caravan and crossed the yard of the red-brick Belgian barracks which housed the HQ. Finding an empty bunk in the officers' dormitory, he fell asleep almost immediately.

The 7th was now moving southwards towards St Vith. The first column had moved off at 4 a.m., the second four hours later. The morning was damp with intermittent drizzle, and the narrow roads were a sea of mud. Many of the officers did not know the route. Maps were not available, the mission was unknown and there had been no time to post guides along the route. But, in spite of the many problems, the division was under way. At first the only trouble, apart from the conditions and the roads, was the presence of German reconnaissance planes. The two-engined Junkers came in low over the crowded columns, dropping flares and turning night into an eerie white-glowing day.

They passed through Verviers. There were large crowds of silent civilians in the streets as they rolled by the big railway station. The soldiers in the armoured car section waved at them and they waved back.

But now rumours started to circulate the length of the column as it began to stall more and more often. The Germans had broken through. They were already back in Belgium. They were certainly heading for a lot more trouble ahead.

Colonel Church M. Matthews, the 7th's chief-of-staff, riding in his Packard and escorted by motorcycle outriders, had just crested the hill at Baugnez on the east route, and had turned down the road towards St Vith, when he drove right into a column of *Kampfgruppe* Peiper. The Germans reacted first. Colonel Matthews's driver was hit. The windscreen shattered and the car skidded to a stop, the driver slumped over the wheel.

Matthews flung open the door. The outriders lay sprawled on the road next to their machines, the wheels still spinning. The colonel sprang across the road and began to run up a hill to his left. A couple of hundred yards away there was a thick clump of firs. If he could get into them, he would be safe. There was an angry shout as the Germans spotted him. Machine-guns stitched a deadly pattern at his heels. Then he was hit. His hands fanned the air as he staggered and fell. The second most important man in the whole of the 7th Armoured's command was dead. Not only that, the east route was now cut. The 7th's advance began to slow down even more.

As it grew light Major Boyer arrived at the hamlet of Poteau with his driver. They were the advance party of the Combat Command Reserve. Here the major knew they could join the main highway running to St Vith from the west. Suddenly the driver jammed on the brakes. The highway ahead was packed solid with vehicles, and they were all heading away from St Vith!

Boyer was horrified. This was no convoy. It was a retreat. He got out of the jeep and walked over to the traffic jam. He saw an officer with a yellow and blue divisional patch on his shoulder, which he didn't recognize.

'What's your outfit?' he asked.

'The Hundred and Sixth Division.'

'What's the score, then?' the major asked.

'The krauts. At least six panzer divisions. Hit us yesterday!'

'What are you going to do about it?' Boyer snapped.

'*Me,* I'm leaving.'

Boyer opened his mouth to say something, then changed his mind. He doubled back to his jeep.

'Move over,' he commanded and slipped behind the wheel. He

swung the jeep into the nearest field which seemed the only way he would get anywhere. Behind him, on a road now cut by Peiper, the 7th Armoured was stalled altogether. Time was running out for the men in the Snow Eifel.

3: Schoenberg

They had just celebrated mass in the little church in the middle of the village. Now the men, dressed in rusty black, congregated in the square puffing at their pipes before going across to the *Gasthaus* for a beer. In the *Gasthaus* Fräulein Schmitz was worried. An American had just told her that the Germans were only two miles away. She had asked him if the Americans would take the civilians with them if they moved back. The American had shaken his head. Now through the window she could see an American sniper climbing the tree above the little grotto dedicated to the Holy Virgin, just beyond where the road from Auw to St Vith meets the one coming down from Bleialf. Fräulein Schmitz decided that it wouldn't be long before the Germans attacked.

In the square the farmers could hear gunfire coming from the direction of both Auw and Bleialf. They looked at each other, an unspoken question in their eyes. Should they flee while there was still time, or take to their cellars? After all, most of them had been born German and a hundred of the village's 300 men were serving in the German Army.

In the fir above the grotto, the American sniper opened up with his machine-gun. The Germans came into sight. A burst caught the sniper, sawing the top of the fir off and flinging him to the ground below.*

The grenadiers stormed forward. They captured the vicarage but the men of the 106th flung them out again. A wounded American was brought into Fräulein Schmitz's house. Then a German soldier burst in. At gunpoint he forced the young American outside and into the barn opposite. Half an hour later, when Fräulein Schmitz dared to venture outside again, she found the American in the barn, *dead*.

* One can still see the topless fir to this day above the grotto.

Now the lower half of the village was completely in German hands, but the upper half, a cluster of houses near the road running up the heights to Bleialf, grouped around the ruins of the eleventh-century castle, was still held by the men of the 106th. Then slowly the firing from up there began to die away, as if the Americans were withdrawing towards Bleialf. The Germans busied themselves cleaning up their half of the village, which controlled the road towards St Vith. Looking through her window, Fräulein Schmitz could see the triumphant grenadiers, mostly teenagers, everywhere. Suddenly she became aware of a strange 'droning in the air'. She shot a quick glance to the bend in the road which led to Auw. Something very heavy and very fast was heading straight for the village.

Major Arthur Parker's 589th Artillery Battalion had fought off all the enemy attacks from Auw the previous day. Now it was clear that the battalion would have to withdraw down the road to Schoenberg which led on to St Vith. Without the covering infantry of the 422nd the gunners could not hold out long against a determined German infantry-tank attack from Auw. So Major Parker gave the order to withdraw.

Earlier that morning the gunners had destroyed the howitzers of C Battery which, bogged down in their gunpits, could not be hauled out onto the road. Now the artillerymen wrestled with the guns of the remaining two batteries, and prepared for the two-mile ride through the unknown to Schoenberg, which Parker still thought was in American hands. With Major Parker in the lead, the convoy set off, while Lieutenant Wood stayed behind to try and get a damaged howitzer on the road. Desperately he and Sergeant Scannapico, plus eleven enlisted men, manhandled the gun towards the waiting prime-mover, its engine already running. The noise of the approaching German infantry was growing ever louder. In the end they managed it, but Parker was no longer in sight.

'Let's roll 'em!' Wood ordered as he climbed into the cab of the prime-mover next to Sergeant Scannapico. Kroll, the driver, needed no urging. He let out the clutch and the prime-mover began its final journey to St Vith. With the engine roaring, they careered into Schoenberg, past a gaping Fräulein Schmitz, the howitzer bouncing wildly up and down, right into the midst of the grenadiers who scattered wildly. From behind the church a tank emerged, its gun swinging round to fire at the intruder.

'Lieutenant, kraut tank!' Scannapico yelled. Instinctively Kroll took his foot off the pedal.

'Go on!' Wood cried. Kroll put his foot down again and they shot forward.

Wood grabbed his carbine. 'When I yell *stop,*' he cried above the racket, 'hit the brakes!'

Kroll nodded, his eyes on the 75 mm cannon now trained on them. Next to him Scannapico gritted his teeth and waited for the crash.

'Stop!' Wood bellowed. The prime-mover lurched to a sudden stop. The two men in the cab sprang out. To the rear the other men did the same. Private Campagna ran forward. He was armed with a bazooka. He aimed. There was the crump of explosives. The rocket struck the tank with a hollow boom. Suddenly the tank's gun dropped.

'We've got the bastard!' someone yelled. 'We've got him!'

There was no time for congratulations. Next to the smoking church, its roof smashed in by a German shell, a machine-gun began firing.

'Mount up,' Wood cried. 'Let's go.'

The men sprang aboard and roared off towards the bridge over the Our. Once across it they would be safe, on the way to St Vith. Slugs pattered off their armoured sides like rain on a tin roof. Kroll pulled to a stop. Without waiting for orders, Sergeant Scannapico, followed by Private Campagna with his bazooka, jumped out. Seventy-five yards to their right, down a little lane which led to Herresbach, they had spotted another German tank, waiting for them to cross the bridge. Campagna fired and missed. The rocket struck a house twenty yards beyond it, throwing up a great chunk of stone. For some reason the tank didn't answer. Perhaps the gunner had been shaken by the rocket. The sergeant didn't wait any longer to find out.

'Back to the vehicle!' he ordered. They pelted back to the prime-mover. Campagna tossed his bazooka aboard and clambered after it. Sergeant Scannapico was not so lucky. A bullet caught him in the small of the back and killed him instantly.

Kroll moved off again. They cleared the bridge, followed by inaccurate machine-gun fire from the little *Gasthaus* to the right of the road, the last house in Schoenberg. They swung round the corner. Up ahead of them was a slight incline with a sheer rock face to their right and a 6- to 7-foot drop to their left. The primemover gathered speed. As they cleared the rise Kroll's foot crashed down on the brake. Less than a hundred yards away the Germans had built a barrier around a Mark IV tank, and its gun was pointing directly at them.

'Bail out!' Wood yelled, knowing that there was no chance of turning round on that road. Madly the men scrambled for the cover of the nearest ditch. The tank's 75 mm crashed into action. Its gunner couldn't miss. The prime-mover's cab was struck squarely by an armour-piercing shell. Kroll, who had remained in the cab, slumped over the wheel, blood streaming down his face. Wood looked around for some way out of the trap. In his haste Campagna had forgotten his bazooka. The men in the ditch with him were armed only with their side-arms, and the Mark IV was beginning to turn its gun on them.

'What we gonna do, lieutenant?' someone yelled, but before Wood could answer, one of his crew rose to his feet.

'Get down,' Wood yelled, thinking that the soldier had gone crazy, but the man was already raising his hands in surrender. He was not alone. Others started to follow suit. A man next to Wood dropped his side-arm, took off his helmet and raised his hands although he was kneeling and concealed from the Germans.

'Hey, cut that out!' yelled Wood. But to no avail. They were all surrendering now. They had had enough.

Wood, the son of a general on Eisenhower's staff, bit his lip. He hadn't joined the army to spend the rest of the war in a German PoW camp. But what was he to do? He glanced about him. To his left there was no cover, just a patchwork of muddy fields around the Our. To his right and up the slope were thick woods. If he could reach them he would be safe. They seemed quite far away, but Wood was very fit. He'd chance it. As the German soldiers, their rifles held suspiciously at their hips, came forward to take the surrender of the Americans, Wood burst from the ditch and began running up the slope. For a moment the Germans did not react. They had been taken by surprise. Then someone yelled an order and the Germans opened up in a ragged volley. Wood zig-zagged crazily. Twisting and turning as if he were back in the football fields of his youth, he sprinted up the slope, with every German weapon paying him full attention. With his chest heaving, he flung himself into the safety of the dank firs. He had escaped!

But no one else was going to escape down the Schoenberg–St Vith road that day. A Major New, the assistant intelligence officer of the 7th Armoured, who had discovered immediately after his arrival at St Vith that the 106th was completely lacking in real information about what was going on on the key link-up road with the two regiments on the Snow Eifel, decided to go and find out for himself. He didn't get far. He had just passed through the hastily erected defence barrier, manned by engineers, when he ran into trouble. German tanks and infantry had blocked the road. Swinging his jeep round, he scuttled back to St Vith to give General Jones his bad news. The road to Schoenberg was definitely in German hands. *The 8000 Golden Lions of the 106th on the heights were finally trapped.*

4: In the Snow Eifel

At dawn the 18th *Volksgrenadier*'s 293rd Regiment on the left flank of Hoffmann-Schoenborn's division swung into action. With considerable *élan* they hit the key town of Bleialf which they had failed to take the previous day. This time the scratch force of the 423rd holding the town could not hold the enemy. Fighting desperately, they were pressed back slowly but surely down the winding road that led to Schoenberg, soon to be in the hands of their comrades coming in from Auw. Enemy armour was swift to follow. They cut through the weak US rearguard. In first gear the tanks and assault guns began to ascend the steep, twisting slope. The American retreat was now in full swing. Cavender's scratch force either surrendered on the road, or, peeling off into the wood trying to escape the tanks, disappeared into the firs back to their parent organization.

The grenadiers made full use of the confusion that now prevailed on the road. A convoy of captured American trucks, filled with armed Germans, infiltrated the American stragglers. A fleeing American armoured car spotted the fact that the trucks were no longer in US hands. The gunner didn't hesitate, although he knew that by opening fire he would give himself and his mates away. He pressed the button of his machine-gun. The truck lurched into a ditch, smoke pouring from its engine; German soldiers sprawled everywhere.

But when the 106th Reconnaissance Troop, to which the armoured car belonged, tried to follow Cavender's radioed advice to 'make your decision' and find a way out of the trap, they found all exits blocked. In the end they destroyed their vehicles and, breaking up into small groups, tried to escape to St Vith cross-country. Only fifty of them made it. Most of their comrades surrendered without any further fight. Thirty minutes later the left and right wings of the German 18th *Volksgrenadier* Division had joined up at Schoenberg. Now the two regiments on the heights were completely encircled, with all known exit roads in German hands.

By nine o'clock that Sunday morning both Cavender and Descheneaux knew they were cut off; but they were more confused than concerned. Except for the flanks, they had seen no action and had suffered few casualties, or so they thought. The hours passed slowly, with the staff officers in both CPs waiting for some word from General Jones. But Descheneaux wasn't idle. He was already beginning to work out a perimeter defence for his CP at Schlausenbach and virtually every officer he could spare was on patrol— on probing missions, contact missions, or simply looking for a way out of the trap.

About midday Descheneaux received his first message for nearly twenty-four hours from Jones. It came over the artillery radio network, because the direct radio link with St Vith was cut, so it had taken a long time to reach the 422nd. But it was very encouraging. It read: 'Supplies to be dropped vicinity Schlausenbach tonight.'

It was just the kind of good news the regiment needed. They hadn't forgotten after all. Enlivened by the news, Descheneaux contacted Cavender over the one remaining line between the two regiments and asked, 'What are you going to do?'

Cavender wasn't sure. His right flank was completely up in the air now. The 106th Reconnaissance Troop had vanished for good, though before they had gone they had reported that there was no way off the heights.

'Jones says withdraw from the present positions if they become untenable,' he replied at last. Descheneaux frowned. Cavender was much older and had had some combat experience, even if it was over twenty years old. 'I don't know,' he said reluctantly. Then he made up his mind. 'Until division tells me definitely to move, I'm staying right where I am.'

'So am I,' Cavender said, conviction in his voice now, perhaps encouraged by the younger man's determination. It was a decision that he would regret many times in the months and years to come —in the camp at Hammelburg when his younger officers spat in his path and refused either to salute him or to take his orders until the camp commandant had been forced to intervene on his behalf; at the courts of inquiry and the inquests in Washington; the years of bitter recriminations.

But that Sunday there seemed other things to do than try to force a way out of the trap before it was too late. He began to swing his battalions round in a perimeter defence, as Descheneaux had done. In addition, he ordered a count of his casualties. They were heavier than he had thought. Whereas the 422nd had only forty wounded who needed evacuation, he had two hundred and twenty-five men killed, wounded and missing. Before he had time to consider his losses, however, another message was received over the artillery network from General Jones: 'We expect to clear out the areas west of you this afternoon with reinforcements. . . . Withdraw from present positions if they become untenable. Save all transportation possible.'

Cavender looked at his watch. It was just after two. He had been right after all to decide to stay put. The relief force was on the way. *This afternoon,* General Jones had assured him. In a couple of hours' time he could well be out of these damned woods and enjoying the first warm meal he had eaten in forty-eight hours. He got on with the business of preparing his perimeter, now confident that everything would work out well. What Colonel Cavender did not know was that Jones had sent that message at 0945 when he was sure it would be only a matter of minutes before the 7th Armoured arrived. The message had taken six hours to reach Cavender, and back in St Vith the first of the 7th's units had still to arrive.

5: Decision at St Vith

At that moment General Jones was having his second talk of the day with General Bruce Clarke.

'Thank God,' Jones exclaimed. 'I've been expecting you since seven.'

'Since seven! General Middleton didn't tell me you were that badly off.'

Jones ignored the remark and plunged straight into the situation in the Snow Eifel.

'I want you to attack Schoenberg. Two of my regiments are cut off on the Eifel. You've got to get them out of there. When can you attack?' He looked up at the brigadier.

'I can't say.'

'What *do* you mean?'

'I came on ahead,' Clarke explained, seeing the look of disappointment on Jones's face. 'I don't know when my men will arrive.'

That had been at ten o'clock. Now it was two in the afternoon and the first of the 7th's units had still not arrived. Both generals were virtually without commands. Clarke had four men under him and Jones had a scratch defence force around St Vith numbering about 500 men of all arms. So the two of them talked about Jones's recent attempt to get an air re-supply for his trapped Golden Lions. According to the 8th Corps air liaison officer the 9th Troop's carrier command at Welford, England, had already been alerted to drop food and ammunition that night.

It was just then that Colonel Devine came in. An hour before Devine and his 'eggs in the basket' had been ambushed on a back road. Devine had abandoned the other officers, turning over command of what was left of the ill-fated 14th Cavalry once more to

Colonel Dugan, who himself would be relieved before the night was out, and, muttering something about 'checking with HQ', had departed for St Vith.

'The Germans are right behind us,' he told the two generals. 'They've broken through in the north. My group is practically destroyed.'

It wasn't the first time that Clarke had seen men crack up in combat, but he restrained an impulse to tell the colonel to pull himself together. He didn't like what he had seen since he had arrived at St Vith. As is recorded in the School of Armor's booklet on the fight at St Vith, most of which he wrote himself:

It was obvious that the shock of the initial German blow, together with their lack of combat experience, had partially disrupted the staff functioning of the 106th. All kinds of rumours were being spread; men who had fled from the front, apparently seeking to justify their action, gave an exaggerated and inaccurate picture of what was taking place. The situation most certainly was bad and the impression that the officers of CCB got was that the 106th no longer existed as an effective division.*

Clarke felt that the best place for people like Devine, who had lost their nerve, was in the rear, where their panic could not affect the already very shaky 106th officers. Therefore, before General Jones could speak, he said quickly, 'Why don't you send the colonel back to Bastogne? He could report the situation to General Middleton.'

Thus Colonel Devine departed the battlefield for good. He had been in combat for two days and he had failed. Now he was going back to the rear to face disgrace and dismissal.† Devine was the first of many good officers who lost their nerve at St Vith. The 'breakdowns' were not over yet by far.

But at that moment Generals Jones and Clarke had no more time to waste on Colonel Devine. To the north of the town heavy

---

* *The Battle at St Vith: An Historical Example of Armor in the Defense,* US Armor School.

† The official US history of the battle is discreetly silent about Colonel Devine. Other commentators say he suffered a 'nervous breakdown'. Merriam, the Ninth Army's historian, who was present at the battle, writes unequivocally: 'The group commander withdrew his troops without orders from the 106th Division, for which he was relieved.'

firing had broken out. American guns were in action. Both men dashed up to the roof of the CP. The first assault column of the 18th *Volksgrenadier* was probing the defences of St Vith, coming up the Schoenberg road and the gap left by the 14th Cavalry. An American spotter plane had seen them sneaking in through the woods just in time and a heavy barrage now descended upon them. For the first time that day the Americans were lucky. A chance shell struck the leading assault gun and stopped it in its tracks. It was fortunate for the defenders—500 men under the command of Colonel Riggs—since their defences were paper thin and they had no real anti-tank weapons. The German column came to a halt and a moment later they were running back into the woods from which they had emerged. The 18th *Volksgrenadier*'s attack on St Vith had been stopped for the time being.

Standing on the roof of the Klosterschule as dusk began to fall, Jones looked at Clarke. His eyes asked the unspoken question, *'Where are the 7th Armoured?'*

It was 1515 hours when an exasperated Major Boyer at Vielsalm, eleven miles to the rear of St Vith, learned that General Clarke had ordered the 31st Tank Battalion of the 7th Armoured to launch an attack east of St Vith to relieve the two trapped regiments early that afternoon. But at that moment the tankers of the 31st were still struggling to get their Shermans through the mob of fleeing 106th and 14th Cavalry men.

Boyer commandeered a 30-ton Sherman and began to storm his way through the chaos. A weapons carrier refused to get out of the way, so Boyer ordered his driver to charge. The carrier driver didn't hesitate. He swung his vehicle into the ditch and the Sherman rumbled on. A command car filled with high-ranking officers tried to nip into the space. Boyer jumped in front of it, arms outstretched, daring them to run him over.

'Get back!' he cried. 'I don't give a damn who you are! Nothing's coming through unless it's going to the front.'

Now the 31st's column began to move slowly eastwards. They had been told, 'Take no orders from any officer, regardless of rank, unless he wears the 7th Armoured patch. If anyone gets in the way, run over him!'

All the same it was to take the column three hours to cover the last two and a half miles to St Vith.

It was now four in the afternoon. On the roof of the Klosterschule the two generals without a command watched helplessly as small figures in field-grey started emerging from the woods to their front once more—German infantry probing the St Vith defences.

Jones made a decision. He knew that up to now he had made all the wrong ones. He should have been more aggressive right from the beginning; then when he had realized that the situation in the Snow Eifel was beyond help, he should have ordered his men to pull back. The result was that he had lost his two regiments—and his son.

He looked at Clarke and said heavily, 'Clarke, I've thrown in my last chips. You take over the defence of St Vith.' Clarke hesitated. He could guess what personal anguish Jones was going through. He had seen his division smashed and undoubtedly his career in the Regular Army was finished. Yet Jones was a major-general and he, Clarke, a very new brigadier-general. There was also Hoge of the 9th Armoured Division to consider. Hoge was senior to him and came under Jones's command. But Clarke made the right decision—one which would take him eventually to the head of a great army. From the defeat he suffered here was to come the start of his real career as a general officer.

'All right, I'll take over.'

Down below at the crossroads the chaos had reached its high point. Infantrymen, cavalry, service troops, signals were all battling their way westwards. The Germans were 'a mile back', 'a couple of hundred yards', 'round the next corner'. A traffic control officer appointed by Clarke to check the panic-stricken mob was simply swept aside by a command car filled with senior officers. In despair the officer sent a man to Clarke to appeal for help. So the new commander of St Vith abandoned all else and, pushing his way through the throng, personally took over the direction of the traffic. A brigadier-general doing the job of a military policeman!

Meanwhile the 7th Armoured's commander, General Hasbrouck, arrived from Bastogne with his new chief-of-staff, Colonel

Refugees fleeing from the battlefield as the Americans first drive into the Ardennes hills in September 1944

●

(left) An American mortar position near St. Vith

Well-equipped and confident of victory, German troops push forward. The film from which this and the following two photos were taken was later captured by the Americans.

●

(below) "The Germans are coming!" Early morning, December 16, 1944—the attack begins.

Victorious German troops pose in front of a captured U.S. "Greyhound"

●

(below) German attackers advancing past a burning American half-track

Obersturmbannführer Jochen Peiper, whose SS battle group led the successful breakthrough to the north of the 106th and commenced the encircling movement which led to the destruction of that division

A German Tiger tank rolls past POWs of the 106th Infantry Division

●

German soldiers looting boots from dead GIs

GIs of the 106th head for the POW camps

A destroyed American 105-mm howitzer

This memorial to the fallen of the 106th Infantry Division stands in St. Vith

●

The mood of the German Army revealed by a sign found by U.S. troops just before the battle. It asks "Victory or Siberia?"

Germans dressed in GI uniforms to act as saboteurs and spies for SS Colonel Skorzeny's commandos are executed by an American firing squad.

Ryan, after a journey which had taken them five hours. A hasty conference was called. It was obvious now that the 31st's counter-attack planned for that afternoon was out of the question. There was still no sign of their Shermans. The relief of the two regiments in the Snow Eifel would have to be postponed till the morning when the 31st Tank Battalion and the 23rd Armoured Infantry Battalion would attack along the St Vith–Schoenberg ridge and break through to the heights. Jones's strained face showed some relief. Hasbrouck was going to do something at last to save his men. Clarke, for his part, frowned. It was a chancy business at the best, especially as the divisional artillery had not arrived to support the attack. The tanks and infantry would have to go in along one road in the semi-darkness without covering fire. Clarke didn't like it one bit but he kept his peace for the time being. After all, in spite of his new command, he was the most junior of the generals present. The main question still was—when would the 7th arrive?

It was dark when the first Shermans of Colonel Erlenbusch's 31st Tank Battalion were led into St Vith by Major Boyer. Clarke met them, standing at the crossroads.

'Take the Schoenberg road,' he yelled above the roar of their motors. 'Go east till you contact the engineers!'

Lieutenant Dunn, the leading platoon commander, transferred to a truck, to reconnoitre for a position for his tanks. But he never reached the supposed roadblock held by the men of the 81st Engineers. A mile east of St Vith he spotted a company of German infantry and three tanks moving towards the town. He swung the truck round and, issuing radio orders to his men, clambered back into his own Sherman.

The Germans and the men of the 1st Platoon, A Company, 31st Tank Battalion met head-on at a bend in the Schoenberg–St Vith road. The fight was short and at point-blank range. The three German tanks were destroyed one after another. The Shermans' machine-guns mowed down the unprotected infantry. The Germans broke and fled back the way they had come. The Battle of St Vith had begun.

Back at St Vith, General Jones, given new energy by the arrival of the first units of the 7th Armoured, prepared his first real order for the trapped regiments since the battle had begun two days before. It read:

> Panzer regtl CT on Elmerscheid*–Schoenberg–St Vith Rd, head near St Vith. Our mission is to destroy by fire from dug-in positions S. of Schoenberg–St Vith rd. Am, food and water will be dropped. When mission accomplished, move to area St Vith–Wallerode–Weppler. Organize and move to W.

At last the 422nd and 423rd had been given a concrete mission.

6: Der Kessel†

As darkness fell on 17 December 1944, there were some 9000 troops bottled up in the heights above Schoenberg. In addition to the 422nd and 423rd Regiments, there were elements of two artillery battalions, engineers, signals, medics and what was left of C Company, 820th Tank Destroyer Battalion.

On one side of the Bleialf–Schoenberg road Colonel Descheneaux had formed a defensive perimeter with its centre south of the village of Schlausenbach. On the other side of the road, Colonel Cavender of the 424th had done the same on the high ground around Oberlascheid and Buchet, where months before Hemingway and Colonel Lanham had eaten their festive dinner in such high spirits. Thus the nine thousand Americans were trapped in an area of six by four and a half miles, with the roads all round them in German hands. The Germans had the mobility the roads afforded them, but there were plenty of tracks in American hands leading north to Schoenberg, though most of them were unsuitable for vehicles. In general there was no shortage of ammunition, for the riflemen and the mortar crews had a basic load of mortar bombs still at their disposal. There was one further day's K-ration available; but there was a shortage of surgical supplies though casualties were not high, and the 590th Field Artillery Battalion had only about 300 rounds left for its 105 mm howitzers.

* He probably meant 'Amelscheid'.
† Literally 'the kettle', in the military sense 'a pocket'.

All in all, the situation of the trapped men was not too desperate. They had food, ammunition and most of the regimental vehicles still intact; and they were not overburdened with wounded men. In the German army, such a *Kessel* was regarded as a normal military way of life. Sometimes 'wandering pockets' (*Wanderkessel*) had progressed for months across the wastes of Russia, living off the land and fighting their way to safety under similar and worse conditions than those which faced the 106th. Indeed *Obersturmbannführer* Peiper had won his Knight's Cross in February 1943 for having escorted one such 'wandering pocket' twenty miles through the heart of a Soviet army which had trapped it—and he had been burdened with over 1500 wounded men! Of course Peiper and his SS troopers were hard and experienced soldiers and the Golden Lions were green and unused to combat, but there was more to it than that. The young men trapped on the freezing heights of the Snow Eifel that night had been let down by the military machine which had snatched them from their homes only a few months before. It had not turned the carefree habitués of drugstore counters, drive-in movies and baseball games into real soldiers, with that pride in themselves and their unit which is known as *esprit de corps*.

In many ways their opponents, guarding the roads around them, were just as young and green. But the grenadiers had confidence in their leadership at all levels, from General Lucht down to the humblest *Feldwebel,* and this confidence gave them a feeling of certainty, of belonging, a knowledge that their leaders and their comrades would not let them down in action.

The Golden Lions had neither pride in themselves nor confidence in their leadership. The US Army had failed to turn them into soldiers, as it was to fail again a quarter of a century later in another field of action, when the men who were now majors and colonels had become two, three and four star generals.* On the morrow the men in the pocket were to pay dearly for that failing.

* Notably General Creighton Abrams, commander-in-chief in Vietnam, to whom General Clarke turned over his command of 4th Armoured Division in November 1944. Also General Westmoreland, Abrams's predecessor; both were colonels at the time of the Battle of the Bulge.

Down below in Schoenberg, Manteuffel himself had arrived to see what progress had been made in the attack on St Vith, which he had hoped to have captured by now. In the abandoned vicarage he conferred with a weary General Hoffmann-Schoenborn. Manteuffel was not interested in the fate of the men in the *Kessel*, who were only four kilometres away from Schoenberg. He was concerned with the capture of St Vith the following morning. Leaning over the map spread out on the priest's table, he explained his plan. The 18th *Volksgrenadier* and the other division of Lucht's corps, the 62nd *Volksgrenadier*, would close on St Vith before dawn. On the 19th the corps would assault St Vith. To lend strength to the 18th *Volksgrenadier*'s attack, Manteuffel would release the newly formed *Führer Begleit* Brigade, an armoured formation under the command of General Remer, to Hoffmann-Schoenborn. The latter brightened up when he heard the news. Remer, he knew, was a jumped-up upstart who made his reputation the previous July, when, as a major in the Berlin Guard Battalion, he had helped to crush the *Wehrmacht*'s attempt to get rid of the Führer. But his new brigade, formed from the Führer's own guard, had been excellently equipped by a grateful Adolf Hitler. It would provide the additional muscle he needed to carry out his mission.

Manteuffel, finished with his briefing, now decided to see what the situation in Schoenberg was for himself. Slipping into an almost ankle-length coat with a fur collar, he left the vicarage. It was cold outside. The wind was blowing straight from Siberia, or so it seemed. For a while he watched the troops moving forward through the muddy street, getting into position for the great attack of the morrow. Behind him in what had been a dance hall, the divisional surgeons in their white rubber overalls worked without pause, sawing off the limbs of young grenadiers, trying to patch them up so that they might live till they reached the rear hospital at Prüm. But Manteuffel did not heed such things. In five years of war he had hardened himself to the misery of battle; a commander could not allow himself to be weakened or influenced by the suffering of the men under his command. He crossed the little bridge over the Our, where Sergeant Scannapico had been killed, and climbed over a fence into the muddy fields, thinking that he'd be able to get ahead quicker that way than on the narrow road leading to St Vith.

As he walked on, deep in thought, he bumped into another man almost as small as himself. He at once recognized the gross-looking, be-monocled officer as Field-Marshal Model, who had also come to have a look at the situation for himself. The two men, who had both enjoyed meteoric careers since 1939, did not like each other very much and their conversation was desultory. Both were preoccupied with their plans for the morrow—how to remove the thorn of the 7th Armoured which stood in the way of their capture of the key road and rail junction.

Still, at the moment they were the victors, and it seemed as if nothing could stop them in the morning. They had broken the 106th Division. At dawn, a whole corps plus an armoured brigade would strike the single division, which was not yet assembled in anything like its full strength, in St Vith. They couldn't fail.

The two men walked on for a while. The noise of the battle had died away, save, in the distance, for the steady rumble of the guns, the ever present background music to battle.

'I'll turn off here, *Herr Generalfeldmarschall,*' Manteuffel said. 'Good night.'

They shook hands and Model said, 'Good luck tomorrow.'

Four:
Decision at St Vith
Monday, 18 December 1944

'Certain of my units, especially the 106th, are broken.'
General Middleton to General McAuliffe, 18 December 1944

1: Adolf Hitler's bodyguard are here!

The first indication for Colonel Fred Warren, acting head of the Combat Command R, newly arrived at the St Vith perimeter, that he'd already been outflanked by the enemy was the arrival of a lone soldier who staggered into his HQ outside Recht. He was bareheaded, bleeding from a face wound and almost incoherent. But he wore the triangular patch of the 7th and was not attempting to run away like the rabble of the 106th and 14th.

Warren sat him down and listened to what the soldier could tell of his story. It was little and confused, but it was enough. The man was Colonel Matthews's driver. He had not been killed at the ambush but had escaped this far. German troops were everywhere, and on their collars they wore the gleaming silver runes of the Armed SS. Somewhere to the colonel's front, the SS were already in occupation!

Colonel Warren sent the driver back to HQ at St Vith with instructions to ask for infantry reinforcements; he would need them now to defend himself. At the same time he ordered the 17th Tank Battalion under Lieutenant-Colonel Wemple into Recht to find out just what the situation was. But Wemple would have to be careful. He must not get bogged down with his Shermans in the village. Without infantry the 30-ton tanks with their highly inflammable petrol engines were easy meat for Germans, armed with their feared *Panzerfaust*. It was not for nothing that the tankers called their very vulnerable Shermans after the famous British lighter, 'the Ronson'.

So Wemple set off into the unknown.

A week before the offensive had started, farmer Peter Schaus of Recht had been suspicious of the strange 'Americans' who had driven into the village in a jeep, looking for 'quarters'. They had spoken broken German with him, but he noticed they had not conversed in English with each other. They had not shown too much interest in the empty houses he had shown them in his official function as deputy burgomaster, and when they had left they had rewarded him with a cigar and not the customary Lucky Strike or Camel he usually received from *Amis*. He thought that perhaps they were deserters from the front, trying to find some quiet place like Recht to hide from the 'white mice', as the local populace called the American military police on account of their white steel helmets. There were plenty of *Ami* deserters about, living off the black market or even by armed assaults on their own convoys, threatening the predominantly coloured drivers to get what they wanted in the way of cigarettes and food.* Now on the morning of 18 December, Schaus knew he had been wrong. The same 'American' soldiers who had been there the week before came back; but this time they clicked to attention in front of him and thrust out their right hands in the well-known 'German greeting'. Moments later they took off their American outer clothing. Underneath were the familiar camouflaged tunics of the SS! Colonel Hansen's 1st SS Panzer Division, the 'Adolf Hitler Bodyguard', had arrived at the St Vith perimeter.

Four tanks of the SS Reconnaissance Battalion, accompanied by Hansen's panzer grenadiers, set off to 'feel out' the American positions. They soon bumped into a jeep from Wemple's 17th Tank Battalion. The men in the jeep opened fire first. One grenadier fell dead, another wounded. A Sherman appeared. This time

---

* The author himself experienced one such 'raid' when Allied deserters raided the barracks in which he was housed that winter. At gunpoint they forced the supply clerks to hand out blankets, highly prized on the black market for the making of coats.

the German gunners were quicker. The Sherman, true to its nickname, went up in flames as the first German shell hit its rear sprocket, broke its track and set its engine on fire. Three American prisoners fell into German hands.

Now a special assault unit of thirty panzer grenadiers pushed across country to attack Poteau, known to be in American hands. Here they bumped into the last survivors of the ill-fated 14th Cavalry, under Lieutenant-Colonel Dugan. The well-trained SS men easily threw them back and Dugan gave the order to retire down the road to Vielsalm, though not all his men obeyed that order; some stayed to fight. Three armoured cars, two jeeps and one light tank disengaged and scuttled to the rear. Later that day Colonel Dugan was relieved of his command, and what was left of the 14th Cavalry was placed directly under the 7th Armoured.

Hansen sent in his mighty Tigers to follow up his grenadiers. Watching from behind their houses, the awed civilians could see how the 72-ton monsters, with their 88 mm guns against which no Sherman's armour was proof, worked their way through the woods towards Poteau. But for once something went wrong with the German attack plan. When they were about 150 yards from the American positions they fired their smoke grenades prior to attacking, as was their usual tactic, and brought their massive guns to bear. The Americans opened up but their shells bounced off the Tigers' steep, heavily armed glacis plates like ping-pong balls off a wall. Then, just as the German gunners were about to fire, they ran into a bog. Tracks spinning wildly, mud and dirt shooting everywhere, the Tigers backed out and tried to reach the Recht–Poteau road. Again they ran into a bog. The first tank sank up to the axles; the second managed to reach the road, but its running mate threw a track at the same instant and the attack faded out.

Alarming reports were now flooding into the *Klosterschule* CP from all around the hastily established perimeter. *'Enemy penetrations at Hunnigen'*, *'Infantry-tank attack coming in at Wallerode'*, *'German column on the Schoenberg'*. On three sides— north, south and east—the Germans were sending in strong probes, according to Manteuffel's plan of the previous evening, trying to find the weak spot in the American defences, where he could throw in the full weight of his forces the following day. Clarke, who had not slept more than an hour all night, didn't need to be told by Intelligence that German strength was growing by the hour. By now 7th Armoured Intelligence had identified both Lucht's corps and the 1st SS. Clarke knew that they were heavily outnumbered in St Vith.

At 0645 he spoke to Colonel Ryan. The problem was the two trapped regiments of the 106th. Was the 7th now in a position to do anything about them? Colonel Ryan, who was new to his job as chief-of-staff, was hesitant to make a decision alone. After all, the corps commander, General Middleton, had given the divisional commander, General Hasbrouck, orders to help Jones out.

Clarke was not so impressed by authority. He was a realist who knew the value of St Vith and its location. He advised Ryan to point out to General Hasbrouck that he still had the option of cancelling the attack on Schoenberg.

In the end it was the enemy, not a command decision, which forced the final abandonment of the plan to try to break through to the 422nd and 423rd. By eight o'clock that morning it had become abundantly clear that the 7th Armoured itself was fighting for its existence; it was no longer in a position to carry out that kind of offensive operation. General Hasbrouck cancelled the attack. The Golden Lions were on their own at last. Now they would have to make their own decisions. It was either *fight or surrender*.

2: This mission is of the gravest importance to the nation

Jones's message of the previous night reached Cavender's HQ at 0730. He and his men, camping out in the freezing woods for the second night, were not very happy. Half the night they had been awake, waiting for the expected air re-supply promised them the previous afternoon. But it had not come. Little did the infantrymen know that Jones's request for air support was still at First Army's HQ. It wouldn't be granted 'appropriate action' (as the military jargon of the time had it) until midday, by which time the two trapped regiments were hopelessly lost in the forest.

But, in spite of their cold, their hunger and their fear of what was soon to come, the staff officers of the 423rd set about preparing a plan of attack. As Cavender saw it, the two regiments should advance down the steep hill to Schoenberg, the six individual battalions abreast of each other, the two regiments linked by a single patrol. In his case, Cavender's 1st Battalion, commanded by Colonel Craig, would be on his left; the 2nd Battalion (under Colonel Puett) on the right, with Colonel Klinck's 3rd Battalion in the centre. In Descheneaux's case, his 3rd Battalion under Colonel Thompson would be on his left and closest to Cavender's regiment, with Colonel Scales's 2nd Battalion in the centre and Major Moon's 1st Battalion on the right wing.

Cavender's plan envisaged the six battalions, with the two regiments abreast, moving off west at ten o'clock and attacking from the south side of the road between Schoenberg and St Vith. In this way Schoenberg, known to be well defended, would be by-passed. It was an awkward and ill-conceived plan which made no consideration for the terrain. Barred from the roads, the two regiments would have to take to the tracks leading south, descending a steep ridge, crossing the Ihrenbach stream, once the German–Belgian border, climbing another ridge of 1500 feet before finally descending another steep slope to the Schoenberg road. In such thickly wooded and rugged terrain, made even more difficult by the deep snow, the men could easily get disorganized and lost. On the narrow forest trails there would be little room to manoeuvre and with some 9000 men jammed into the area, confusion and firing upon one's own troops seemed inevitable, especially as there was no overall commander of the operation and only the single patrol link. It was no wonder, when Colonel Descheneaux received Cavender's message that they were to attack, that he bowed his head and said to his operations-and-intelligence NCOs, Sergeants Loewenguth and Wayne, *'Oh, my poor men—they'll be cut to pieces!'*

The order to move was passed down the chain of command. Heavy equipment was broken up by sledge hammers. The kitchen trucks of the service companies were destroyed by pouring petrol over their tarpaulins and hoods and setting them alight. The firing pins of the 57 mm anti-tank cannon were screwed out, smashed against rocks and flung away into the snow. In the case of the

423rd Regiment, the wounded were given over to the care of medical orderly volunteers. They were to be left behind.

Now under a leaden sky, the dirty, unshaven men started to move out. Behind them the wounded in the regimental aid station shouted their encouragement.

There was a nightmarish quality about the long columns of men, emerging from the valley and descending the slope into the woods. They spoke little, each man wrapped in his own thought.

Colonel Descheneaux took the point of the 422nd main column himself. His mood of despair had vanished. He, too, had been affected by the unreal quality of the morning, but instead of making him sluggish, it appeared to make him light-headed. Perhaps it was because he was going into action for the first time.

'You're crazy, colonel,' his operations officer gasped, as they started up yet another wooded slope, deeper and deeper into the unknown. 'You're going to get yourself killed!'

Descheneaux shook his head. 'I've got to be sure we're going in the right direction,' he said.

Behind him the Golden Lions plodded forward, up and down the steep hillsides, blindly following their leaders, concentrating only on the feet of the man ahead of them, concerned solely with keeping going.

The assembly area for the 422nd's part of the attack on the supposed German panzer regiment on the Schoenberg–St Vith road was four miles away. But as the terrain was so tough and visibility down to 200 yards, only slow progress was made. Soon the parallel trails* were littered with overcoats and gas masks, usually the first pieces of equipment to go.

'We abandoned everything,' Captain Roberts of D Company recalls, 'except our weapons and ammunition. Ammunition was low and there was no food or water. There was no straggling. Stops were made every few minutes as the advance guard searched every foot of the terrain. No shots were fired in the vicinity of the column where I was.'

Indeed there were no shots fired at all in the 422nd area that

* From the American position down to the Ihrenbach stream in the valley there are myriad parallel trails which run together and sometimes vanish altogether once they hit the stream.

day. Colonel Descheneaux ended his first day of combat in fifteen years of service with his hands as bloodless as they had been at dawn; he saw no Germans, nor did he fire his personal weapon.

By midday the lack of knowledge of the terrain and the bad weather was beginning to tell. Men started to go astray and some got lost—either accidentally or deliberately—for good. Some of the officers began to regret they had ever set out on this wild attack to their own rear. They should have remained in their secure, well-established positions in and around the Siegfried Line and fought it out. By late afternoon, the 422nd Infantry Regiment was lost.

Like the 422nd, Cavender's 423rd destroyed its kitchen equipment and left its wounded behind at the regimental collecting station as it set off on the road that led through Oberlascheid and Radscheid to Schoenberg. Colonel Puett's 3rd Battalion took the lead and ran smack into the Germans an hour later.

An H Company weapon-carrier, emerging on to the Schoenberg–Bleialf road, was confronted by one of the grenadiers' roadblocks, covered by an 88 mm cannon. Its first round smashed into the carrier at close range. The impact was so great that the carrier was blown right on to its back, its front crumpled up like a peeled banana. Privates Fischer and Spencer crawled out of the smoking wreckage in a daze. It didn't last long, however. They grabbed the carrier's 50-calibre machine-gun, which was undamaged, and turned it on the German crew. Surprisingly enough they fled their well-prepared position, leaving the two Americans in possession of the cannon.

About this time T/4 William Dienstbach and T/5 Watters were captured by the Germans. The enemy sat them on the front of a captured jeep and, keeping them covered with their machine pistols, drove at full speed for the 423rd positions, using the two American NCOs as a human shield. Just as the jeep reached the 423rd, the two captives screamed 'Germans!' at the tops of their voices, simultaneously flinging themselves off the bonnet into the snow. The men manning the 423rd position didn't hesitate. The jeep driver took a machine-gun burst in the chest. Seconds later the jeep smashed into a ditch. The remaining Germans surrendered.

Now, with the aid of his mortarmen, working their 81 mm mortars until the tubes glowed red, Puett made good progress, pushing the grenadiers back towards Bleialf, opening a path for the rest of the regiment.

Cavender went up to see the situation for himself, but he never reached Puett. En route he received another radio message from Jones in St Vith via the artillery network, saying that the 7th Armoured's counter-attack had finally been abandoned. The two regiments should now attack Schoenberg.

Cavender passed on the message to Descheneaux, then ordered Colonel Klinck's 3rd Battalion to come up on Puett's right and help him out in the drive for their new objective. At noon Puett sent an urgent plea for help, but none was forthcoming. Colonel Klinck's 3rd Battalion had carried out Cavender's order well enough. They had advanced across the Ihrenbach stream and ascended the steep hillside beyond, reaching a spot about a mile from Schoenberg. There they dug in, having lost contact with both their own regiment and Colonel Descheneaux's 422nd.

Cavender ordered up his 1st Battalion. They would clear out the woods astride the Bleialf–Schoenberg road and make things easier for the hard-pressed Puett, but the 1st ran into trouble right from the start. The Germans were well dug in in the thick beech woods on the other side of the road. Lieutenant Thompson rushed two enemy machine-gun posts. Then, grabbing a bazooka, he went tank-hunting. But his luck ran out. The Germans spotted him, machine-guns opened up and he fell, badly wounded. Soon after this the 1st Battalion's commanding officer, Colonel Craig, died of his wounds. Two hours earlier, when Cavender had been giving him his orders for the attack, the air had been rent by the howl of incoming artillery.

'It sounded like every tree in the forest had been simultaneously blasted from its roots,' Colonel Kelley, CO of the 589th Artillery, recalled.

Nagle, Cavender's executive officer, had fallen, wounded in the back.

Now Colonel Craig was dead, the steam started to go out of the 1st Battalion's attack. To their right, Puett's advance began to peter out, too. The psychological moment had passed. The 1st and 2nd Battalions started going to ground, exhausted by the march and the fight, too tired to dig foxholes in the frozen earth, oblivious to everything but the desire to close their eyes and ears, to see and hear nothing more. The only thing that was going to get the men on their feet again was hot food and drink. Colonel Cavender was thinking the same. That morning he had suffered over 300 casualties, including sixteen officers; he simply couldn't afford to lose so many leaders. He was well aware after two days of complete confusion that his battalions could well disintegrate for lack of leadership. Anxiously he scanned the grey sky. Surely the promised air drop must come soon.

Away in St Vith that afternoon, Colonel Brock, the 106th's G-3, followed up General Jones's message to Cavender with one of his own, dispatched at 1445. It read:

> Attack Schoenberg, do maximum damage to enemy there. This mission is of the gravest importance to the nation. Good luck. Brock.

The words would have been farcical if the situation on the heights had not been so tragic.

3: A general departs

About the same time that Cavender's attack was finally stalled St Vith was suffering its second major attack of the day from Lucht's corps and the 1st SS. The pressure on the 7th was too much; Clarke's screens to the east, facing Schoenberg, started to withdraw even further away from the trapped regiments. At Steinebrück, where the Ihrenbach stream meets the River Our, the last bridge, which had been kept open in case the 423rd might be able to retreat across it, was blown up by a platoon of the 9th Armoured, while under enemy fire.

Now the attacks on St Vith were coming in all along the perimeter.

At Poteau a massive tank battle had started which lasted over seventy-two hours, to become the greatest tank battle in US military history.* The Adolf Hitler Bodyguard threw in its Panthers

---

* Perhaps not in terms of the number of tanks involved, but in the length of engagement. Villagers in Recht remember how every night for four nights, twenty or more German tanks would go into the line, coming back in the morning laden with casualties. One SS NCO was shot for attempting to destroy his tank.

and Tigers against which Clarke's Shermans had only two advantages, their electrically operated gun turrets and their speed. Otherwise they were no match for the German tanks, which outgunned them, outweighed them and possessed much thicker armour. Still the Americans fought back with a spirit which enabled them to hold Poteau against everything the Germans could throw at them until they were finally ordered to retreat.

By mid-afternoon Clarke saw that his position in St Vith was no longer tenable as a command headquarters and decided to withdraw to the village of Crombach to the south-west of the town. But the problem of Jones was an awkward one. Could Clarke, as the overall commander of St Vith, order Jones, a major-general, to withdraw to the rear? Besides Jones was beginning to irritate him. While Clarke, like the little Dutch boy in the story, was trying to plug up new holes which appeared everywhere in the dyke of his perimeter, Jones still plagued him to attempt to make an attempt to rescue the 422nd and 423rd.

The staff of the 106th Division, for their part, were also eager to see their commanding officer move to Vielsalm and set up a new CP next to General Hasbrouck's. But General Jones hung on, waiting desperately for some news of the air drop which he thought was already taking place. Indeed that morning he had contacted Colonel Towne, the VIII Corps's air liaison officer, personally and had asked for a 'further' drop. By this time the 435th Troop Carrier Group, at Welford in Buckinghamshire, had finally been alerted. Loaded with parapacks and door bundles, the DC 47s had set out for Florennes, Belgium, where they would be briefed on the op and be given fighter cover—twenty-three planes in all, flying through the fog blanketing the Channel.

While Jones waited anxiously at his CP, the DC 47s were told Florennes didn't want them. 'Too busy to take you,' the tower radioed. 'Why don't you go to Liège?' The group commander and another pilot landed all the same. They found the field totally unprepared for them. There was no briefing, no map coordinates, and no fighter cover! While they argued with the Florennes base commander, the rest of the 435th Troop Carrier Group was diverted to Dreux Field near Paris. And there they remained until their mission was finally cancelled on 22 December. By then the men of the trapped regiments were either dead or long vanished from the heights.

At 1450, as there was still no word from Colonel Towne at corps HQ, General Jones finally gave in. His division had virtually vanished. There was no need for him in St Vith anymore. With the hand grenades still unused in the tray, the man who would 'never be taken alive' sat slumped in the back seat of his car as his driver set off for the rear.

4: All quiet in the pocket

As General Jones's Packard rode down the single road which still linked St Vith with the rear, the commanders on the Snow Eifel used the cover of darkness to organize themselves for the morrow. Having lost touch with the 423rd during the afternoon, Colonel Descheneaux set off towards the sound of the guns, firing to the west and north-west. He was still to all intents and purposes lost, but the gunfire did enable him to guide his men through the darkness to three small woods above and facing the Bleialf–Auw road. He knew the road was in enemy hands so he ordered his exhausted men to bed down there for the night. They would cross the road and descend to the Ihrenbach stream below at dawn.

Meanwhile Colonel Cavender had disengaged his other two battalions to support a dawn attack by Colonel Klinck's 3rd Battalion, which was in the best shape. While the 1st and 2nd had run out of mortar bombs and machine-gun ammunition and were low on rifle ammunition and rounds for their bazookas, Klinck's battalion, which had suffered few casualties, still had plenty of ammunition.

Cavender had just formed a semblance of a defensive perimeter on Ridge 536, south-east of Schoenberg, the highest point in the wooded area above the village, when he received Colonel Brock's message. It had taken eight hours to reach the 423rd and it infuriated some of his officers, when he read it out to them in the cover of a freezing dugout. They thought its clumsy appeal to patriotism insulting and unnecessary. The 423rd would carry out its mission without the need to be urged on by such hackneyed cliches as 'the gravest importance to the nation'. It was their job to fight and fight they would; they didn't need canteen commando clap-trap like that to make them do so.

Cavender ignored their reactions. He only had eyes for the worn, dirty faces of his exhausted men and the wounded lying in the far corner of the lantern-lit dugout, their eyes dilated with drugs or screwed up with pain. Most of them had not had a drop of water or a bite of food all day, while they had marched and counter-marched through some of the most rugged terrain in north-western Europe. Now they were at the end of their tether. He recognized the signs. He had been a doughboy in the trenches in the First World War and he knew the sufferings the average footslogger had to undergo well enough from personal experience.

In retrospect it is easy to criticize the two commanders responsible for what the official US military historian has called the 'most serious reverse suffered by American arms during the operation of 1944-45 in the European theatre'. Why weren't they more aggressive? Why did they wait so long before they acted? Why did they rely so much on orders from General Jones in St Vith, when they knew the situation in the Snow Eifel much better than he did? General Bruce Clarke's 7th Armoured men showed that men in combat, confronted with a sudden and confused situation, could act aggressively, immediately and independently.*

Perhaps the two colonels, though both were professional soldiers, did not have the 'will to win'. They were, perhaps, prepared to sacrifice their careers, their futures, their personal pride because they *felt* too much for their battered soldiers, little realizing that nothing, even the promise of life, would be able to erase the stigma attached to what was to come. Unlike the bespectacled Major Whittelsey of the famed 'Lost Battalion', who, when cut off in the Argonne Forest in France in 1918, refused to surrender and lost most of his battalion in the process, they set their faces steadfastly against such final measures. They refused to accept

---

* Because the 7th was thrown into action piecemeal as it arrived at St Vith and because radio communications between each unit were so tenuous, it was up to each commander to rely on his own initiative. In virtually every case these commanders, senior and junior, reacted with dispatch, energy and force.

such overwhelming casualties. When the choice was finally between surrender and death Colonels Descheneaux and Cavender both chose the former.

Just before midnight Cavender started giving his orders. The staff officers flipped open their pads and, as best they could in the hissing white light of the Coleman lamp, scribbled down his instructions. Runners began to leave the dugout CP bearing instructions to the battalions. Weary NCOs roused their men out of the undergrowth. Weapons clinked in the dark. Slowly the exhausted infantry began to move out down the hill. Men collided with each other as they stumbled on through the freezing darkness. The Golden Lions were going in for the last attack.

On the roads which surrounded the pocket, the young grenadiers waited at their posts, stamping their feet in the cold, blowing their frozen hands to restore some life in them, cocking their heads to wind every now and again, trying to catch the faintest sound from the dark mass of the woods to their front.

There weren't many of them—the 293rd Infantry Regiment, a single battalion of field guns and the newly arrived 669th *Ost-Battalion,* made up of ex-Red Army PoWs, officered by Germans. But they were confident. They controlled the roads. Soon the *Amis* would have to come out of the woods and face them.

Five:
Surrender in the Snow Eifel
Tuesday, 19 December 1944

'In war the moral is to the physical as three to one.'

Napoleon

1: Objective Disaster

As dawn broke on the 19th, it revealed the battered 423rd Infantry Regiment lying huddled behind the saddle of Hill 536.* Down below, barely visible in the dawn mist, lay the village of Schoenberg. The weary, befuddled men rubbed their red-rimmed eyes and stared down at it numbly. This was their objective.

Colonel Cavender began checking his battalions. Colonel Puett's 2nd Battalion was on the reverse side of the hill to the right; the 1st Battalion, which Craig had commanded, was to the rear; Klinck's 3rd, with which he had set up his own command post, was on the hill, nearest the Bleialf–Schoenberg road.

His men were down to about a half of their original strength and they were in pretty bad shape. But the skies were beginning to clear and he prayed that today they would get an air drop, which would put heart into them again. Shortly before nine o'clock, Cavender called a conference of his officers.

'We will attack at 1000 hours in column of battalions,' he told his dirty, unshaven officers. He turned to Colonel Klinck, whose 3rd Battalion had taken the smallest number of casualties. 'You're in the best shape. You'll carry the burden of the attack.'

Klinck nodded. His battalion would come down the exceedingly

* The number indicates the ridge's height in metres. Its height, therefore, is roughly 1700 feet.

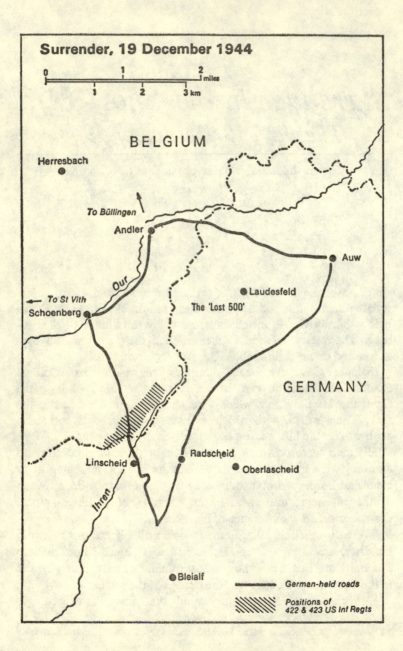

Surrender, 19 December 1944

BELGIUM

Herresbach

To Büllingen

Andler

Our

Auw

To St Vith

Laudesfeld

Schoenberg

The 'Lost 500'

GERMANY

Linscheid

Radscheid

Oberlascheid

Ihren

Bleialf

——— German-held roads

///// Positions of
422 & 423 US Inf Regts

0   1   2   miles
1   2   3 km

steep logging track from Hill 536 to where the road, descending into Schoenberg, made a 90-degree bend. Here they would be hidden from whatever German troops there were in Schoenberg itself. All they would have to contend with would be the enemy on the road, and with luck they could deal with them and rush down into the village before the Germans were aware of what was happening. At all events, from now on at least they would be going downhill.

Cavender, precise, formal and a little old-fashioned right to the end, glanced down at his watch, prior to co-ordinating the time with his officers. 'It is now exactly nine o'clock. . . .'

He never finished his sentence. Suddenly the morning air was torn by the sound of incoming shells. The group around him stiffened.

'Look out!' someone shouted, but before the officers could throw themselves to the ground, shells were striking the firs all about them. Fist-sized, red-hot steel fragments scythed through the trees. The sole German field artillery battalion along the Bleialf–Schoenberg road pounded the command post, sweeping the whole length of the south-eastern slope of Hill 536 and, behind the covering fire, the grenadiers attacked. They came in from the rear, easily overrunning the 590th Field Artillery, gunners without guns, and other scattered service units, which had formed up behind the rifle battalions. The artillerymen started to surrender. Now Cavender's rear was cut off. There was only one way for him to go—forward.

But at that moment he had other problems besides the surrender of the 590th Field Artillery to his rear. The thirty-minute artillery bombardment had completely demoralized his command post staff. Clerks, runners, and headquarters defence GIs cowered in shallow holes and behind the firs and refused to get to their feet when the first sergeant bellowed, 'Move out!' Like frightened rabbits they had gone to ground and would not move.

'*Move out!*' the enraged sergeant yelled. But for once the angry bellow had no effect. Officers from Cavender's staff came up. But no amount of cursing or threatening seemed to have any effect on the demoralized men. Lieutenant-Colonel Nagle, Cavender's exec-

utive officer, wounded in the back and in pain, was equally un-
successful.

At this moment a very large negro corporal stalked in from the
trees with a tommy gun tucked under his arm, as if he were going
for a morning stroll. He seemed absolutely unconcerned by what
was going on around him.

'Colonel, sir,' he said in a thick southern voice. 'You all seem to
be alone here. I'm from the 333rd Field Artillery. Anything you
want me to do?'

Colonel Nagle clutched at straws. There was no time to be
wasted. The Germans were at their heels. He nodded his head at
the cowering men.

'Get this platoon organized, corporal,' he said gratefully. 'Move
north, covering our flank.'

Colonel Klinck's 3rd Battalion moved off smartly. They came half
stumbling, half running down the steep logging trail from Hill
536. Captain Huyatt's company was in the lead. They came to the
bend in the narrow Schoenberg road and ran straight into a German gun position—an 88 mm cannon, covered by twin-barrelled
40 mm anti-aircraft cannon being used in a ground role.

The attack disintegrated as the gunner manning the twin cannon
fired at the Americans. Captain Huyatt yelled above the racket for
his men to take cover. But to one side of the road there was a
deep drop and to their right the bank was too steep for them to
climb into the better cover of the trees. So they lay on the road or
in the right-hand ditch, pinned down by the deadly white tracer of
the shells just above their helmeted heads.

Then Huyatt heard the unmistakable sound of tank tracks. He
raised his head and saw, down below in the valley, a tank beginning to crawl towards them. There was no mistaking that high
glacis plate. It was a Sherman. He turned his head to the men in
the ditch around him.

'It's one of ours!' he cried. This was the armoured relief they
had been promised, arriving at long last.

Next moment the Sherman fired, an HE shell whistled through
the air and erupted above them, sending shrapnel hissing through
the trees. They buried their faces in the dirt. The Sherman was in

German hands. It rattled past and the German 40 mm cannon-fire began to slacken. Perhaps the tank crew thought they had eliminated the *Amis* who had appeared so suddenly from the trees. Captain Huyatt didn't know or care. He had other problems now. He could hear the sound of many men coming through the trees behind them—Germans. He pulled out half his remaining company to repel them. Firing from the hip as they ran, Huyatt and forty men charged up the track down which they had come. Many GIs fell but their charge worked. The Germans coming through the forest began to withdraw.

Absolutely exhausted, the survivors of Huyatt's charge collapsed in the foxholes they had dug on the summit of Hill 536 the previous night and took stock. The lead company's situation was bad. There were about thirty riflemen and fifteen men armed with the BAR light machine-gun left. They were cut off from the other two companies of the 3rd Battalion, which had struck out for Schoenberg further down the road and were down to perhaps one clip of ammunition per man.

An hour later, at 1130, the Germans attacked again. They rushed Huyatt's position from all four sides. The Americans held out for only a few minutes before their ammunition ran out. There was nothing more they could do now. As the triumphant grenadiers swept up the slopes, firing as they came, GIs began to raise their hands or take off their helmets in token of surrender. By now the Germans knew and recognized this strange *Ami* token of defeat. The firing began to die away. More and more riflemen raised their hands. Huyatt dropped his carbine and rose to his feet.

The attack of Klinck's 3rd Battalion also failed. At 1300 hours, perhaps some seventy minutes later, Klinck ordered his two surviving companies to withdraw and begin digging a defensive perimeter. It was the last they ever dug.

The 1st Battalion of the 423rd Regiment set off under command of Colonel Craig's executive officer. The major had no real knowledge of Cavender's plan of attack, but he pushed forward on the 3rd's left, unaware that the Germans were closing in on both sides with tanks and infantry. In spite of the fact that the lead company had lost its company commander, two platoon leaders and several riflemen in the initial barrage, the 1st Battalion made good progress. Indeed it looked as if they might be lucky after all.

Then, like the 3rd, they ran into a concentrated barrage of German anti-aircraft guns used in the ground role. The attack came to an abrupt halt. Men fell dead and wounded everywhere. Platoon leaders tried desperately to rally their men, but to no avail. Nobody was prepared to face the solid wall of fire coming up from the enemy positions. Tanks began to emerge from the trees. B Company, unable to go either forward or backward, was surrounded.

The remaining two companies fled to their original positions. B Company stayed where it was and fought it out, until, as the official history of the 106th Division has it, it was 'eliminated'.

Colonel Puett's battalion, which had suffered the most casualties in the fighting of the previous day, moved out fast but, located on the extreme right of Cavender's regiment, was soon separated from the other two battalions. Undeterred, Puett's men pushed on and came out on the east of Schoenberg. Now reports started coming in to the battalion HQ by runner that more and more Germans were being spotted where they shouldn't be—some 400 yards to the battalion's right.

Before Puett had a chance to investigate, firing had broken out on his right flank. Eager for revenge after the beating they had taken the previous day and thinking, for once, they had taken the Germans by surprise, the 2nd Battalion's riflemen poured in all they had. Yells of pain and cries for help told them they were finding their targets.

Suddenly a bareheaded soldier broke from the trees where the 'Germans' were located. His eyes wild with fear, his hands raised in surrender, he yelled, 'Don't shoot! Don't shoot!'

The 2nd Battalion men dropped their weapons. The soldier facing them was wearing khaki. They had been firing at Colonel Descheneaux's men.

By two o'clock that day Colonel Cavender knew that his last attack had been a disastrous failure. He had lost a large number of men, killed, wounded or captured. All his artillery had been overrun, and his hungry, dirty, exhausted riflemen were down to a clip of ammunition per man. Next to his own CP, the regimental surgeon, Major Fridline and his staff were swamped with casualties they simply could not attend to in the primitive conditions of their dugout.

But most important of all, Colonel Cavender knew that he had lost tactical control over his regiment. What was left of them was split up into isolated groups in the forests all around. The end was near for Colonel Cavender's 423rd Infantry Regiment.

2: *Vielsalm*

Back at their CPs in Vielsalm, General Hasbrouck and General Jones took stock of their situation that Wednesday morning. To Hasbrouck everything at St Vith, eleven miles away, was confused. His 7th Armoured Division was positioned in a great arc around St Vith and Vielsalm. The northern half, under Bruce Clarke, didn't worry him too much. He knew Clarke for the great fighter he was; he would take care of things there.

It was the southern half, beginning just below St Vith, which worried and confused Hasbrouck. This section was nominally under the command of his fellow general in Vielsalm, Alan Jones, and it was definitely very shaky. Consisting of General Hoge's Combat Command B of the 9th Armoured Division and Colonel Reid's 424th Infantry Regiment of the 106th, the two regiments were not only separated, under German attack, running out of food and ammunition, but they were obviously also the weak point von Manteuffel had been searching for all the previous day. Von Manteuffel knew it by now, as did Hasbrouck. But did Jones? On the 18th, General Middleton's last words to Hasbrouck had been, 'You and Jones carry on up there.' As Hasbrouck interpreted Middleton's words, they meant that he and Jones were in equal command of the St Vith salient. Hasbrouck was worried about Jones. In turn, he seemed numb, overcome by the shock of what had happened to his regiments and to his son, and then completely unrealistic, wildly optimistic, apparently unaware of the gravity of the situation. Did he now realize that the German force reported assembling at the small town of Gouvy in his sector was possibly the forerunner of an all-out attack by von Manteuffel? If not, could Hasbrouck, joint-commander and yet junior to the major-general in rank and age, order Jones to do something about it?

At eleven o'clock, at about the same time that Captain Huyatt of Klinck's 3rd Battalion found he was cut off, Hasbrouck, still undecided what to do about Jones, was disturbed by the entry of an exhausted infantry colonel into his office. The newcomer introduced himself as Gustin Nelson of the 28th Infantry Division's 112th Regiment which had originally been located to the 106th's right flank on the day the offensive had begun.

'What are you doing way up here?' Hasbrouck asked in astonishment. 'And where the hell's the rest of your division?'

Nelson shrugged. 'Don't ask me, general. I just found out where *I* was this morning when I ran into one of your patrols.' Colonel Nelson explained that he had lost contact with his division and had been wandering about the countryside all the previous day. Although he had not suffered too many casualties, his riflemen were hungry and tired.

But Hasbrouck wasn't worried about the state of Nelson's men. They were bodies, exactly the bodies he needed to plug Jones's gap. He telephoned the general and suggested straight out, 'Why don't you attach Nelson to the 106th?'

He explained that the 112th could be plugged into the gap between Hoge's 9th Armoured and Reid's 424th. This way, Jones would have a solid front. The arc would then be a complete horseshoe which might deter von Manteuffel from pressing home his attack there. General Jones accepted with alacrity. He didn't seem in the least concerned about the fact that a junior brigadier-general was telling him, a major-general, what to do. It was the best bit of news he had received since the offensive had started three days before. Now he was actually in command of something more than the 500-odd bodies which had been in his charge back at St Vith. He had three units directly under his command.

General Hasbrouck put the phone down and breathed a sigh of relief. He knew he would have to make most of the decisions in the St Vith command. As he wrote after the war: 'I never knew who was in my command. I just did everything I thought necessary. The command status was more or less an assumption.'

For his part General Jones retreated into his strange dreamlike world of wishful thinking once more. Perhaps if St Vith could hold, now that the perimeter had finally firmed up, his two regiments would be able to fight their way back to the besieged border town. There was still hope.*

3: Surrender!

At about the time Colonel Nelson left Hasbrouck's office in Vielsalm, Major Moon of Colonel Descheneaux's 1st Battalion ordered his C Company to cross the road that leads from Auw to Bleialf. The road runs along a high ridge and is clear on both sides of trees. But at regular intervals on the far side there are tracks leading into the woods which fringe the Ihrenbach stream in the valley below.

Moon surveyed the road. There were no Germans in sight and, knowing that the tracks on the far side would allow his men to move to the nearest cover without having to bunch and present an easy target for the German artillery somewhere on the road leading to Schoenberg to his left, he made his decision.

'Move out!' he yelled. The leading company broke cover. At that same instant, four German tanks emerged from the woods to his left and began firing. Tree bursts and HE showered the frightened GIs with splints of wood and steel. The first platoon took their lives in their hands. Crouched low, weapons held at the port, they doubled across the road. They cleared it and ran all out for the cover of the trees fringing the Ihrenbach stream below.

The rest of the 1st Battalion hesitated. Colonel Descheneaux hurried up and tried unsuccessfully to co-ordinate the crossing. Enemy fire now broke out from the woods to the 1st's right. They were being hit from both flanks. The scared riflemen went to ground.

One of the survivors of that crossing, who found himself in a small valley which turned sharply to the right and got smaller and

---

* Right up to the day when he was finally relieved General Jones seemed to believe that his regiments in the Snow Eifel were still fighting. As late as 22 December an attempt was made to reach the 423rd Regiment by radio. By then it was deep in the heart of Nazi Germany.

smaller as it ran to the ridge road, remembers, 'Small groups of men were trying to cross the road when tanks began filling the opening of the valley with fire.' That was bad enough. Now, however, the Germans pushed in another tank.

'It pulled up behind us,' the survivor remembers, 'and began to fire at the other end. The slaughter at the end of the valley by the road was bad.'

D Company, which had gone to ground like the rest, set up a 50-calibre machine-gun and began to fight back. German infantry were advancing across the open fields towards them and they presented a choice target. But not for long. The German guns zeroed in on the American defenders. An 88 mm shell exploded right behind the machine-gun team and they disappeared in a ball of red flame.

A bazooka team, crouched low, doubled across the fields towards the leading German Mark IV. The aimer hoisted the long tube on his shoulder, while his loader fumbled with the rocket. But the two brave men never fired their weapon. German machine-gun fire scythed them down as they stood there in the open field.

'We loaded,' another bazooka man remembers, 'and got ready to fire. When I saw several of our own men walking towards the tanks with their hands up, I saw it was useless to fire because I was sure we would kill all those men. We broke up our weapons and surrendered. There were two hundred and fifty in this group.'

Major Moon didn't wait to see that surrender. He had seen enough already. Rising swiftly to his feet, followed by his staff and a few brave men who wanted to fight on, he pelted across the road and down the steep slope to the woods beyond. The 1st Battalion, 422nd Infantry, was finished as a fighting force.

To Moon's left Colonel Scales's 2nd Battalion had also come under fire as they crossed the high ridge road from Auw to Bleialf. They had taken a few casualties but had pressed on, heading north-east through the forests.

The leading platoon came out of the wooded heights to see down below them the winding Bleialf–Schoenberg road, which led to their objective. The anxious looks on the riflemen's begrimed faces changed to ones of joy and relief. Down below, the narrow winding road was packed with vehicles. Bumper to bumper they ground their way forward. Surely this must be the relief force they had been promised for the last three days? The Germans didn't have that kind of transport.

'Don't fire,' an officer cried. 'They're friendly vehicles.'

Tanks began to work their way awkwardly around the nearest bend, while the hidden watchers followed their every movement. Again the word passed from mouth to mouth. 'It's our armoured breakthrough. . . . They've come to pull us out.'

Suddenly one of the black-uniformed tank commanders spotted the dirty men crouched on the hillside above the road. He reacted quicker than they. His gunner opened up immediately and HE shells began to drop among the weary GIs. By ill chance, Colonel Scales's battalion had bumped into the tanks of Major-General Otto Remer's *Führer Begleit* Brigade, which Manteuffel had promised Hoffmann-Schoenborn two nights before. Due to the traffic jams everywhere in Germany, they had taken all this time to arrive at the battlefront.

H Company's mortars and machine-guns were knocked out by the concentrated fire almost immediately. The battalion started to take bad casualties. But still they fought back. Staff-Sergeant Almond, angered beyond all measure by this terrible blow to their last hopes and the casualties they were taking, rolled a hundred yards down the hillside without being hit. Standing there, breathless and muddy, in full view of the Germans, he mowed down the crew of a German spandau. Up above him with the one surviving mortar, Corporals Dorn, Madsen, Brouch and Snovel laid down a deadly barrage of 81 mm bombs on the German vehicles. Three of the German self-propelled guns, whose tops were open and which could not manoeuvre on the narrow road, were knocked out in rapid succession. But the German fire was becoming too much for the men on the hill. Twice-wounded Lieutenant Walker of H Company dragged together what was left of the 2nd Battalion and plunged back into the woods.

A few minutes later he took a break and allowed the exhausted men to get their breath back after the hectic flight into the trees. He took the opportunity to count the survivors. There were 199 men of 15 different outfits. That was the end of the 2nd Battalion's attack.

Colonel Thompson's 3rd Battalion was luckier than either of its sister battalions. Finding some sort of a gap in the German positions, they filed through the woods towards the third of the roads which led into Schoenberg, the one from Andler. Suddenly one of the riflemen spotted shadowy figures in the fog-bound firs to the left. The riflemen didn't wait for orders. They opened fire at once. From their left a ragged volley returned their fire. Suddenly someone spotted that the men were in khaki like they were. They had been firing on Colonel Puett's 2nd Battalion of the 423rd Infantry!

Slowly but surely Colonel Descheneaux's attack ground to a final halt. The woods were full of confused, demoralized men, who were rapidly running out of ammunition and hope. Behind them the foxholes and dugouts were filling up with more and more casualties. Now the German infantry began to leave the roads surrounding the American positions in the woods, while the tank guns and those of the field artillery covered them. A heavy silence fell on the Linscheid Forest. The end was near.

It was now nearly 3.30 in the afternoon, Colonel Descheneaux had pulled his battered command into the shelter of the deep woods overlooking Schoenberg. By now the Germans dominated the battlefield. For the Americans it had become a matter of survival, nothing more. In a last attempt to do something, Descheneaux sent out scouts to search for escape routes. Those few who managed to return reported that there were none. The enemy were in full control of every track leading out of the woods.

Packed into an area of less than two square miles, the 422nd were sitting ducks. The Germans fired into them at will and they had no defence. They began taking more and more casualties. Two gunners, Kelly and Lackey, staggered into the 422nd's positions. Both of them had had their outfits—590th and 589th Artillery—overrun by the Germans to the rear. They reported to Descheneaux that Colonel Cavender's battered 423rd Regiment, 1000 yards from the 422nd, was in a similar position—surrounded and ready to give up.

Descheneaux called a conference of his officers in the 20-foot-long trench which served him as a CP. Together they tried to make sense of the rumours and counter-rumours which were running from foxhole to foxhole. For a little while they were cheered by the rumour that the tanks of the 7th Armoured had reached them on the road to Andler, just below the woods. But when they, too, turned out to be those of Remer's brigade, having lost their way and turning back towards Germany and away from Belgium and St Vith, most of them lost heart for good.

Colonel Kelly records:

The krauts were closing in slowly and there was heavy machine-gunning to our front and left—some shelling from our right. We had nothing but 30-calibre—no food, medicines or blankets. The latter items were worst because there was a steady stream of wounded from the gully to our west and without dressings or blankets there was nothing we could do except let them lie in their gore and shiver—with the most goddam pitiful look in their eyes. I put my coat over one—when it was all over, I felt like a heel going back for it—but he didn't need it anymore. The situation was hopeless.

Now, as Descheneaux explained the situation to his officers, these same wounded and dying flooded the next dugout, which was the regimental aid post, crying out in pain and calling repeatedly for water. But there was no more water, although there was a whole river of it, the Our, only a matter of yards away. But the River Our was in German hands. Captain Perkins, the commander of Descheneaux's M Company, was carried by two stretcher-bearers. One of his legs had been shot off.

Descheneaux looked around the anxious faces of his officers. He had known some of them for nearly three years. They were part of his wartime life, as much of his adult existence as were his family. He had drunk with them in the officers' clubs, sweated it out with them in the hot summers of the south on manoeuvres, bitched with them about when the 422nd would finally go 'over there'; he knew their wives, their kids, their personal problems. Was he justified in allowing them to be slaughtered like this?

'We're being slaughtered,' he exclaimed, putting his thoughts into words. 'We can't do anything effective.' He hesitated, know-

ing perhaps instinctively that his next words would mean the end
of his military career.

Then he said, 'I don't believe in fighting for glory, if it doesn't
accomplish anything. It looks as if we'll have to pack it in.'

Colonel Kelly was digging a foxhole when he heard from a junior officer what 'Desch' had just said. As we have seen, he was as
concerned as the CO of the 422nd was about the wounded. Now
he dropped his entrenching tool and hurried over to Colonel Descheneaux. As he recalled later: 'The situation was hopeless. But
some of us were in favour of holding out until dark and attempting to get out in small parties. I thought that had been decided
upon.'

Although Kelly knew they 'weren't even a threat [to the Ger-
mans]', he argued with Descheneaux.

'Desch,' he said, 'you can't surrender.'

'No?' the colonel said bitterly and looked at the mounting pile
of dead and wounded next to his command post.

Kelly shut up, knowing that it was no use now. Desch had made
up his mind. Later Kelly stated that, 'If his [Descheneaux's] command post hadn't been the regimental aid station, he could have
stood it a little while longer. He had been right up with the leading
elements in the attack that morning.'

Descheneaux turned to his other officers, some of whom looked
at him with little attempt to conceal their contempt at what they
believed was his weakness, or even worse, cowardice.

'As far as I am concerned,' he said, 'I'm going to save the lives
of as many as I can. And I don't give a damn if I am court-mar-
tialled.'

Someone tried to protest but Descheneaux was no longer listening. 'Break up your weapons,' he ordered. 'Break up your pistols.'

Without waiting to see if his order was being carried out, he
crawled back into the trench and started to cry.

About a thousand yards away Cavender, too, was at the end of
his tether. He knew his regiment no longer existed as a fighting
force, whatever the more pugnacious of his young officers thought.

As Colonel Kelly said of him, 'Cavender was reluctant to take
command without an order.' Now he would have to take command

without orders and make that overwhelming decision. He knew that the decision would mean the end of his military career. West Point had no place in its curriculum for what he was about to do.

At about four o'clock that afternoon, his mind made up, he called a conference of his officers.

'There's no ammunition left,' he told them. 'We're down to a clip per man.'

There were murmurs of concern among those officers present who already realized what Colonel Cavender was going to do.

'I was a GI in World War One,' he continued, 'and I want to try to see things from their standpoint. No man in this outfit has eaten all day, and we haven't had water since early morning.' Cavender paused and then he let them have it. 'Now what's your attitude on surrendering?'

There was a shocked silence.

It was Colonel Nagle, the wounded executive of the 423rd, who volunteered to contact the Germans. Taking a soldier of German origin who spoke the language with him, Nagle descended the hill to the road, the soldier waving a makeshift white flag. Up above the rest waited in gloomy silence.

Nagle returned with a young grenadier lieutenant of the 293rd Infantry Regiment, plus a small number of German soldiers. The German lieutenant couldn't speak English, but he could speak French, a language in which Descheneaux was fluent. The colonel dispensed with the soldier interpreter and dealt with the German directly. Together they began to work out the terms of surrender. Out of the corner of his eye, Descheneaux noted that the Germans were relieving some of his men of their watches and cigarettes.

'Let my men keep at least one pack apiece,' he said.

'Everything will be correct, colonel,' the lieutenant answered and shouted an order at his grenadiers. The negotiations went on.

Cavender's officers were still reluctant to surrender.

'I'm expecting enemy artillery at 1630 hours,' Cavender announced.

'I know it's no use fighting,' one of his officers remarked miserably, 'but I still don't want to surrender.'

Cavender didn't react. 'Gentlemen, we're surrendering at 1600 hours.'

The survivors of the 422nd started to file down the slope onto the road below. As Colonel Kelly saw the hundreds of Germans waiting for them there, he said to Descheneaux, 'You were right, Desch. There was nothing else you could do.'

Colonel Descheneaux nodded dejectedly, but said nothing.

The news that the colonel was surrendering passed from foxhole to foxhole in Cavender's command. The company commander of I Company heard the news from Cavender himself at his CP. He doubled back to his own company and told 1st Lieutenant Collins, his executive, who was digging a foxhole, 'We're cut off. In ten minutes the regiment is going to surrender. Have the men destroy their weapons.'

'What?' Collins cried with shock. 'Did somebody panic?' He received no answer.

Angry and confused, he called the company together and told them what was going to happen.

'Destroy your weapons,' he ordered. He could see that most of the men were glad it was all over. But not all of them. Sergeant Dowling came up to him and said, 'All my men want to break out. Will you lead us, lieutenant?'

Collins debated with himself for a moment or two, then he shook his head. 'I'm sorry, sergeant, the orders are to surrender,' he said.

Not far off 1st Lieutenant Alan Jones Jr, the son of the divisional commander, would not believe the rumours that had begun to go the rounds of the foxholes. Even when the German artillery ceased pounding their positions he still refused to believe that they were going to surrender. When the firing stopped altogether and his men began to wander around in bewilderment, one of the stragglers he had formed into a unit that morning came up to him. He was a big negro artilleryman with a tommy gun, perhaps the same energetic corporal who had rallied Cavender's HQ platoon the previous day.

'We haven't even started fighting, lieutenant,' he protested to Jones. 'Let's go and kill some Germans.'

Just then a runner came up and reported, 'All weapons will be rendered inoperable, sir, and all units will stand fast.'

Jones stared at the runner in speechless disbelief. A few minutes later the triumphant young grenadiers came swarming into the 423rd's positions. The GIs raised their hands. Expertly and swiftly the Germans frisked them, taking cigarettes and wrist watches, but allowing the prisoners to retain photographs and other personal possessions.

But not all the Golden Lions were prepared to surrender that easily. Many brave or desperate men refused to carry out the two colonels' orders. Captain Murray, the 1st Sergeant Rifleman and Private Dickens of the 423rd disappeared into the forest before the Germans came into their position. They avoided the grenadiers till well after dark. Sneaking by the German-occupied village of Setz, they waded through the River Our. They were only a couple of miles from St Vith and safety. In the dark, however, they bumped into a sentry. Before he could fire his rifle, Captain Murray stabbed the German with his trench knife. The thrust was not fatal and the man started to scream. Dickens grabbed him and, slipping his arm round the German's chin, forced his head back and smothered his screams. Now, with the sentry's neck exposed, Murray sawed at the naked flesh. It seemed to take hours before the struggling man finally went limp and Dickens could let go. By the time they had finished, Captain Murray had slashed his fingers into a bloody mess. Shaking with nerves and horrified at what they had been forced to do, the three pushed on and made it to the besieged town.

Next day they went back into the line again at St Vith, with the men of the 7th Armoured.

A Company of the 423rd had been cut off from the rest of the regiment that afternoon. Groping their way cautiously through the snowy forests, they found themselves back at Oberlascheid, almost exactly where they had started from three days before. For a while they squatted there in the snow, wondering what to do next, now that they were so far behind the German lines.

It was about then that Lieutenant Ivan Lang of the regimental I & R Platoon made his appearance. Together with the company commander, Major Helms, he began to lead A Company back towards Belgium. An 88 mm spotted them and shells started to drop around them. Helms and Lang decided to split up, each taking two small parties with them.

Helms never made it, but Lang was more fortunate. With sixty-eight men and two other officers, he managed to get through to St Vith. They were taken to the 7th's assembly point for stragglers at the schoolhouse, where they were fed and questioned. Later, on the night when St Vith fell to the enemy, they were put in the line again.

As Clarke wrote afterwards:

> When they were told that they were going back into the line, their enthusiasm was high, and subsequent reports from the troops with whom they fought indicated that without exception these men discharged their duty in exemplary fashion.

Indeed there were those of the 106th who were still fighting long after St Vith had fallen and General Clarke and his 7th had retreated westwards to Vielsalm.

Lieutenant Fisher Wood had been unable to break through to St Vith. During the night of 18/19 December he had hidden in the house of Peter Maraite in the little hamlet of Meyerode. That night he told M. Maraite that if he—and his companion, a private of the 423rd—couldn't get through, he'd 'collect the Americans who are everywhere in these woods and start a little war of my own'.

On the 19th, Wood began that 'little war'. Soon Meyerode became the headquarters not only of Field-Marshal Model, the overall commander of the attack, but also of Sepp Dietrich, the commander of the Sixth SS Panzer Army. Daily convoys crept through the woods to Meyerode to bring supplies to the two HQs; and daily the smaller convoys were attacked as they took the forest trails.

Although Dietrich's HQ forbade the villagers to go into the

woods, they knew what was going on from Maraite's cousin, Burgomaster Johann Pauels, in whose house Dietrich was quartered.

As they worked it out from statements made by German officers, Wood had established himself with some hundred men from different units of the 422nd and 423rd in the area of the Adesberg Hill, deep in the woods between Meyerode and the road from Schoenberg to St Vith. 'These *Ami* criminals and scoundrels', as the German officers called them, played havoc with the smaller supply columns. Virtually every day the German supply troops brought in wounded men from the woods, complaining that they had been attacked by Americans, led by a young officer 'very big and powerful of body'. Obviously Lieutenant Wood.

How the Americans lived, the villagers didn't know. But they presumed that they subsisted on what they found left in the abandoned American foxholes or what they took from ambushed German convoys. No one will ever know, for apparently none of them survived.

On the late afternoon of 23 January 1945, the same day that General Bruce Clarke returned to a recaptured St Vith, the burgomaster of Meyerode sent his cousin, August Pauels, and Servatius Maraite to look for the Americans, now that the SS men had fled. Everywhere the two men found the grim signs of the slaughter that had taken place in the woods over the last month. They discovered hastily dug German graves in virtually every little glade and unburied Germans in ditches on the sides of most trails—200 in all. Then they found Wood. Servatius Maraite found him in a thicket not far from the spot where six trails meet. Around him lay the dead bodies of seven Germans. All of them had died about ten days before. That no *living* German had been there after Wood had died was proved by the fact that Wood still had his papers and 4000 Belgian francs in his wallet, which surely would have been looted.

Wood had died, fighting to the last, taking with him the last of his opponents. Sadly the villagers buried him at the spot where the six trails meet and on the cross they later erected over the grave wrote his epitaph—ironically, in German.

It reads:

> Eric Fisher Wood
> Capt. US Army
> *fand hier den Heldentod*
> *nach schweren Einzelkaempfen**

Now the prisoners started to stream out of the hills as the triumphant grenadiers drove them from their last hiding places. Jakob Peterges, from the hamlet of Andler which lay directly below Colonel Descheneaux's positions, remembers opening his back door that afternoon:

> I was curious to see what was going on. Opposite my house on the other side of the road in a field there were about two thousand Americans. On my doorstep there was a German sergeant with a film camera. He had a big grin on his face. I realized why. He was photographing the beaten Americans for Goebbels' propaganda service for movie audiences back in Germany. As soon as he'd finished making his film, the guards moved on. The Americans started marching to Auw in Germany and the prisoner-of-war cages.

Innkeeper Kessler, who owns the little inn at the corner where the road from Andler turns off to Auw, recalls that afternoon well enough, too:

> They came in long columns. They were exhausted and very dirty. Some of them were carrying their wounded on ladders and doors—perhaps found in Andler. Some of the officers were taken into my dance hall, opposite the inn, and questioned by the SS officers we had billeted here. One of the SS asked me what I thought of the *Amis* now. I said they'd always treated me well before the offensive. He didn't like that.

Later, one of the grenadiers waiting at Bleialf for the signal to attack St Vith wrote in a typically enthusiastic letter to his family back in the Reich:

> Endless columns of prisoners pass; at first, about one hundred of them, half of them Negroes. . . . American soldiers have little spirit for fighting. Most of them often said: *'What do we want here? At home we can have everything much better.'*

---

* Found a hero's death here after unsparing singlehanded combat.

But the dirty, unshaven, hungry men of the 106th Division were not interested in the German reaction. They were preoccupied with their own lot. Their part in the war was over, ended almost before it had begun. Now they were 'kriegies', as they would soon learn to call themselves in the PoW camp slang (from the German word for prisoner of war—*Kriegsgefangener*).

Between 8000 and 9000 men were in German hands. Robert Merriam, the Ninth Army historian and later head of the Ardennes Section of the Office of War History, was in Belgium at the time. He called it:

> the largest mass surrender of American arms on the Western Front. Both Germans and Americans who have studied the situation since then feel that the troops could have put up a stiffer fight, but they were green, the weather was poor, no air drops were made, and communication was almost non-existent. General Jodl expressed surprise that the two regiments were unable to hold out longer; General Middleton felt similarly.

They had become part of a major Allied defeat in the West. Three months before, the Allies had suffered a major reverse when they failed to hold Arnhem, but when the British 1st Airborne Division knew that its situation was hopeless, it carried out a fighting withdrawal. Out of the 10,000 men who had gone into that battle, 1500 were killed and, of the 6000 taken prisoner, over 3000 were wounded. The paratroopers succeeded in killing or wounding 3300 Germans. These are the German figures.

That was not the case with the 422nd and 423rd Regiments. Their surrender in the Snow Eifel that day 'represents [as the Official US History of the Ardennes Battle puts it] the most serious reverse suffered by American arms during the operations of 1944-45 in the European theatre'.

As that December night drew on, the Golden Lions stumbled down the little border roads deeper into Germany. As they marched east, their mood grew blacker. Everywhere there were signs of a great American defeat. The roads were a mass of abandoned American equipment, mostly from the 14th Cavalry Group —tanks, armoured cars, guns of all calibres, trucks, personal gear— and not all of it had been wrecked by enemy action, or effectively sabotaged by its one-time American owners. Much of it had simply been abandoned in good working order when the troops had panicked and fled for their lives.

Those of the Golden Lions who were not too weary and demoralized grew so angry by the sights all around them that they used their rest periods to unpick their divisional patch. *They* did not want to be associated with such a disgraced division.

Andrew Rooney, a *Stars and Stripes* reporter, records: 'After the battle men tore off their roaring Golden Lion badge . . . and conscientious battle casualties among them wept at the thought they had let the Army down.'

In the midst of this mob the two colonels, Descheneaux and Cavender, marched too. Cavender was already being cold-shouldered by his men and officers. In the PoW camp to which they were heading he was glad when he was relieved as senior officer by the appearance of another American colonel, senior to him; his officers simply refused to obey the orders of a superior they felt had let them and the army down.

Descheneaux marched unrecognized. Earlier that afternoon, just after the 422nd had surrendered and had been formed up into columns by their jubilant captors, an unshaven infantryman from one of his battalions had recognized him.

'I've got a message for you, colonel,' the soldier had said. Descheneaux looked at the man dully and said nothing. Thereupon the soldier had stuck out his tongue and given his CO the Bronx cheer. Descheneaux had saved the man's life and that had been his reward.

Now he marched eastwards with the rest of the mob. Behind him the red and white signal flares rose into the darkening sky over St Vith. General Hoffmann-Schoenborn's full division, now released from the Snow Eifel pocket, was preparing to launch an all-out assault on Clarke's defences in the town. But Colonel Descheneaux did not look back. For him the war was over. He would have the rest of his life to ponder over the decision he had made on 19 December 1944.

Six:
Even Generals Wet Their Pants
Wednesday, 20 December–Friday, 22 December 1944

'After all, gentlemen, you can't win the big victory
without a tidy show.'
Field-Marshal Montgomery to General Hodges and staff,
21 December 1944

1: The 'Lost 500'

On the afternoon of the 19th, when the two regiments began to
surrender to the Germans, fragments of the 422nd's 2nd Battalion
started to drift onto Hill 576, south-west of the German hamlet of
Laudesfeld. Here, to their surprise, they found a haven of peace.
On the top of the hill, a detachment of the 634th Anti-Aircraft
Battalion had formed a perimeter, which had been completely
missed by the attacking Germans.

Around this nucleus, Major Albert Ouellette, the executive
officer of the 2nd Battalion, and Major Moon, who, as we have
seen, had lost his own 1st Battalion, began to collect stragglers
who were prepared to fight. By late afternoon they had some 500
men and about twenty 50-calibre machine-guns. They had plenty
of ammunition and—best of all—food. That evening the 'Lost 500'
had their first hot meal in three days.

By dusk the two majors had organized a defensive perimeter
and had begun sending out small patrols, which soon established

that the 422nd and 423rd Regiments had surrendered. The news did not dismay the two young majors, although they were deep in German-held territory by this time, with the nearest American troops over twenty miles away. By the following day the leading German tanks were within sight of the River Meuse, far to the rear. Their position was good and they were confident they could hold out until help came from St Vith. They did not realize that Bruce Clarke in St Vith was fighting for his very existence; there would be no help forthcoming from that particular quarter. They bedded down for the night and waited.

The Germans, cleaning up the pocket and foraging for supplies, found the 'Lost 500' on the morning of the 20th. After the initial exchanges of fire the Germans, unwilling to suffer further casualties, decided to try to woo the 'Lost 500' into surrendering. In the surrounding trees they hung loudspeakers, blaring out the latest swing music from the States, broken at intervals by tempting offers to surrender and be given as much food and drink as they wanted.

The racket got on the defenders' nerves and affected them more than the bullets. Major Fridline, the 423rd regimental surgeon, who had done such yeoman work over these last few days, finished sewing up a casualty and turned round to see a GI sitting in a ditch, tears streaming down his dirty, unshaven cheeks, yelling, 'Blow it out, you German sonofabitch!'

The Germans were indeed all around the Ouellette–Moon command, and they were edging ever closer to the perimeter. All the while the loudspeakers poured out the ear-splitting music, which contrasted so strangely with the Americans' present surroundings, laced with tempting offers to surrender.

It was too much for Staff-Sergeant Thomas of H Company. Asking for volunteers, he crept out at their head and led them to a little knoll where the enemy sound truck was located. Unsuspectingly, the German English specialists continued with their propaganda. Thomas took a deep breath and prepared for action.

'Now!' he cried. Thereupon, as Colonel Dupuy records: 'Berlin Betty's playful references to the joys of playing baseball in a PoW camp ended with the wham of a well-directed grenade.'

At noon that day a German reconnaissance car, bearing a white flag, crawled cautiously up the road from Laudesfeld towards the

Americans, who followed its progress with fingers crooked around the triggers of their machine-guns, ready for any kind of trickery. The armoured car contained a German medical officer from Schoenberg and a captured medic from the 423rd. The American aid post on a hill above Schoenberg had not been closed by the Germans. Instead German and American medics continued working side by side long after the surrender, tending to the wounded of both sides. The two medics were from this aid post.

The German MO explained, with the aid of the 423rd man, that they would offer them a truce while the wounded of both sides were evacuated. But, while the 423rd man translated, the German took in the real situation on the hilltop position and he changed the offer of a truce to one of surrender. Major Ouellette did not react. He allowed the Germans a truce to clear away the wounded, but, while they were doing so, he sent a spy of his own, Lieutenant Houghton, to have a look at the situation on the German side of the line.

Half an hour later the lieutenant came back and reported that it didn't look good. The Germans were in full strength and were supported now by artillery field pieces. He had learned, too, that the enemy intended to start an all-out attack that night under cover of artillery fire. Their deadline for the attack would be 2300 hours. If the 'Lost 500' had not surrendered by then, the attack would commence.

It was now seven o'clock; they had four hours left. Major Ouellette called an all-officer conference and told the officers what he had learned from Houghton. Should they surrender now? Some of the officers felt that they should attempt to hold out another couple of days. They said there was enough food and ammunition to do so. Perhaps division would still be able to rescue them. Others argued that they had radioed their position to divisional HQ and had received no reply. Perhaps St Vith had already fallen. But the biggest factor in their decision-making was the presence of German artillery. If the Germans used their field pieces at close range, it would be sheer slaughter.

The debate went back and forth, but in the end they had to face up to the inevitable. Major Ouellette sent a message to the Germans, agreeing to surrender on the following morning, once the 'Lost 500' had broken up their weapons.

Thus, at eight o'clock on the morning of 21 December 1944, less than one week after the 106th Infantry's two regiments in the Snow Eifel first went into combat, the last sizeable unit of the ill-fated 422nd and 423rd surrendered. Only 200 of the 10,000 men originally estimated to have been up there in the snowbound hills on Saturday, 16 December had managed to escape the German trap.

SS General Leon Degrelle, the Belgian fascist leader who had been sent to Belgium by Hitler to take over the administration of the eastern region of the newly captured territory, passed through the captured Americans that afternoon on his way to St Vith. He stopped to fill up in Andler and then drove on towards the town, which was already under heavy attack, thinking that what he had seen so far of the Americans didn't show them to be particularly good soldiers. Degrelle, who had joined the SS as a private and had worked his way up to general, complete with the Knight's Cross of the Iron Cross won in Russia, knew real soldiers when he saw them; and the rabble of American prisoners he had come across behind the front had not impressed him one little bit. But that Friday afternoon he was to see another kind of American soldier. Just west of the summit, his driver was forced to stop by the congested traffic heading for the beleaguered city. Degrelle took the opportunity of stretching his legs. In the fields next to the road, he came across a trench:

> In it were dead Americans, lined up just as they had been when they were alive and with their cheeks still pink from good food and exposure to fresh air. Tank fire had mowed them down and two of them had their faces completely flattened but with a noble expression. The trench was full, because every one had stuck to his post, in spite of the wave of fifty or a hundred tanks which had swept up on them, leaving the tracks which I could see in the snow.

Degrelle walked back to his car. He had seen some real soldiers.

2: The last casualty

At that moment complete confusion reigned on the other side of the line in what the American defenders were now calling the 'fortified goose-egg': the egg-shaped defensive line which stretched around St Vith and back eleven miles or so to the headquarters of General Jones and General Hasbrouck in Vielsalm. It was not because of the confused fighting alone, which had seen General Clarke himself imprisoned and held prisoner by his own MPs for five hours.* It had more to do with the command structure.

On 19 December General Eisenhower had appointed Field-Marshal Montgomery to the command of the northern shoulder of the Bulge, making him responsible for Hodges's First Army, to which the St Vith salient belonged. One day later Montgomery had pleaded for a withdrawal from the St Vith area, telling Hodges, 'After all, you can't win a big victory without a tidy show.'

Hodges had been uncertain. It wouldn't look good if he withdrew Hasbrouck's and Jones's men. Hodges's subordinate commander, General Ridgway of the 18th Airborne Corps, who took over the immediate command of the area under the terms of the changeover, was violently opposed to any withdrawal. He reckoned the 7th Armoured should be able to hold out, even when completely surrounded.

Clarke, Hoge and Hasbrouck thought differently. They knew there was not much time left if they were going to avoid the fate of the 106th. Their men were exhausted; they were running out of supplies; and they were opposed by elements of at least four infantry and three armoured divisions. With one real road left leading out of the salient, the commanders on the spot wanted an immediate decision before it was too late. But who was to give it? Nobody really knew who was in charge of the defence of the

* General Clarke had been arrested because, in the generally chaotic situation, the MPs had been told to look for 'a kraut posing as a one-star general', which he was. At the end of this frustrating five-hour term of imprisonment, the MP sergeant had the gall to ask Clarke for his autograph. Clarke was so nonplussed that he gave it.

fortified goose-egg. General Hasbrouck thought he was now in charge. Two days before he had finally received his first decisive communication from VIII Corps HQ, which had been transmitted to Middleton by First Army itself.

It read:

Ridgway with armour and infantry is moving west to gain contact with you. When communication is established you come under command of Ridgway. You retain under your command following units: 106th Division (RCT 112) and CCB 9th Armoured Division.

That had been clear enough for Hasbrouck. The army commander had given him command over Jones and what was left of the 106th Division. To make his position perfectly clear, Hasbrouck wrote a note to General Kean, Hodges's chief-of-staff, stating:

General Jones is a Major-General and I am a Brigadier. His being attached to me makes it look as though he had failed in some respect and I want to put myself on record as saying he is in the saddle in control of his outfit and that we are co-operating in the best possible way. If my note [of the previous day which had caused 1st Army to react for the first time] gave any other impression, I want to correct it at once before an injustice is done.

On a carbon copy of the above Hasbrouck added for General Jones's benefit: 'This is being dispatched at once with a copy to General Ridgway. I hope it will correct any misimpression my note to General Kean may have caused.'

At 0830 on the morning of 22 December, however, both Jones and Hasbrouck received the following message from their new commander Ridgway:

The following msg sent at 0100 is repeated for your information. Confirming phone message to you. The decision is yours. Will approve whatever you decide. Inform Jones he is to conform.
2. In addition to his force Major-General A. Jones will command 7th A. D. effective receipt this message.

The 'decision' referred to in the message from Ridgway was that of whether the 'fortified goose-egg' should be evacuated or not. But who was to make the decision? The army commander, Hodges, had confirmed that Hasbrouck was in overall command. But his subordinate, Ridgway, the man on the spot, had now appointed Jones as commander of the forces in the goose-egg. As Colonel Dupuy wrote:

> The decision to withdraw was left by XVIII Corps [Ridgway] to the commander of the troops in the salient. Just who that was during the morning of 22 December is a question for a guardhouse lawyer to decide. . . . Hasbrouck would make the decision, Jones would conform, but Jones would command Hasbrouck. As puzzling doubletalk it would be hard to beat this fifty-odd word message.

Thus, while the survivors of the 7th Armoured and what was left of the 106th Division's 424th Regiment fought all out to save their skins, knowing that if they weren't evacuated soon they would suffer the fate of Cavender's and Descheneaux's men, the general wrangled, incapable of making a decision. The situation appeared to be the same as during those fateful first two days of the surprise German counter-attack when General Jones had sat on his thumbs and done nothing, while the trap was sprung on his Snow Eifel regiments.

By now the end was near in the fortified goose-egg. Major Boyer's last hundred men who had been defending the rear of the 7th Armoured had just been overrun and captured, including the intrepid major. Now the *Führer Begleit* Brigade was lining up next to the infantry of the 18th *Volksgrenadier* Division to launch a final attack on the one road linking the fortified goose-egg with the rear.

In Vielsalm Hasbrouck wrote a detailed memo to Ridgway, outlining the seriousness of his position to his new corps commander. It began: 'Unless assistance is promptly forthcoming, I believe our present position may become serious for several reasons.' Hasbrouck then outlined those reasons and concluded: 'I don't think we can prevent a complete breakthrough if another all-out attack comes against CCB tonight.'

Hasbrouck had just finished the memo when that all-out attack came. Hurriedly he added a postscript in his own hand:

> PS. A strong attack has just developed against Clarke again. He is being outflanked and is retiring west another 2000 yards, refusing

both flanks. I am throwing in my last chips to halt him. Hoge had just reported an attack. In my opinion, if we don't get out of here up north of the 82nd* before night, we will not have a 7th Armoured Division left. RWH.

Hasbrouck's message reached Ridgway at a few minutes before noon. It arrived half an hour after a telephone message from Jones, the new overall commander, who had stated that he concurred with Montgomery and Hasbrouck: the salient should be evacuated. Now, while Ridgway glowered at Hasbrouck's memo which laid it clearly on the line, an aide brought in another memo. This was from General Jones, but now he had changed his mind. In his memo Jones stated: 'My intentions are to retain the ground now defended.'

It was too much for Ridgway. He had had enough of all this pussy-footing. The situation in Vielsalm was hopelessly confused, or so it seemed to him, and his subordinate commanders lacking in guts. Ordering his jeep, he set off for Vielsalm.

'By hearing their voices and looking into their faces,' he wrote later, 'there on the battlefield, it was my purpose to get from them on the ground, their own sensing of what they were up against.'

At about one-thirty that afternoon, Ridgway arrived in Vielsalm and began his 'hearing of voices and looking into faces' at once; and he didn't like what he heard or saw. Standing in front of the wall map, Ridgway drew a large goose-egg on the map between St Vith and Vielsalm.

'What do you think of making a stand inside this area?' he asked. 'You'd hold out until a counter-offensive caught up with you. You'll soon be surrounded, of course, but we'll supply you by air.'

Hasbrouck replied first. 'I don't like it,' he said. 'The area is heavily wooded with only a few poor roads. Besides, the troops have had over five days of continuous fighting in very trying weather. My people are only fifty per cent effective. And I'm sure that goes for the infantry, too.'

Ridgway didn't like Hasbrouck's answer. He was used to being

---

* The 82nd Airborne Division, once commanded by Ridgway, now part of his airborne corps.

cut off. All the parachute operations he had been involved in in this war had meant he had been cut off for some time; there was nothing problematic about a situation of that kind as long as the Allies controlled the skies, which they did. He looked at Hasbrouck with scarcely concealed disgust. He obviously lacked aggressiveness and backbone.

Suddenly Jones said, 'I think it can be done.'

The remark angered Hasbrouck. The infantryman didn't understand the special problems of a tanker. The fortified goose-egg simply wasn't tank ground. There were too many woods and too few roads, and in that kind of terrain a tank was a sitting duck without an infantry screen.

'Tanks can't manoeuvre in there,' he protested. 'We could only use them as pillboxes.'

Ridgway ended the discussion there. He slapped his helmet on, seized his carbine and snapped, 'Come on, Bob. The two of us will go up front and see just what the hell the situation is.'

Followed by an equally angry Bob Hasbrouck, he filed out, leaving Jones staring at his broad back in open bewilderment.

It was now half past three in the afternoon and Clarke was in the fields just beyond his new command post at the village of Commanster. He was testing the snow-covered ground to check if it would bear the weight of a tank or half-truck. After some time he decided it wouldn't. He walked back to his CP to be told that Ridgway was on his way to hold a commanders' conference.

Impatiently he waited for the arrival of Generals Ridgway and Hasbrouck, knowing that time was running out fast, that a decision had to be made before dark or the positions of the 7th Armoured would be overrun. During the cover of darkness the 7th might be able to make their way through the 3000-yard bottleneck to the westward exit from the fortified goose-egg over the two remaining bridges across the Salm at Vielsalm and at Salmchâteau. By the following morning an operation of that kind would be out of the question.

At four-thirty Ridgway faced the assembled commanders. He looked aggressively at Colonel Reid of the 424th Regiment.

'What's the combat efficiency of your unit, colonel?' he snapped.

'About fifty per cent, sir,' Reid replied.

Ridgway turned to Clarke. Like Reid and all the rest of the officers present, Clarke was an unknown quality to him. For the last two years he had associated mainly with airborne officers, who formed a special elite of their own.

'And yours, Clarke?' he asked.

Clarke didn't pull his punches either. He wasn't that kind of a commander. 'Forty per cent, sir,' he answered promptly.

Ridgway frowned. After what he had seen during these last two days in the Ardennes, he was beginning to suspect everybody's motives and courage. He had been forced to arrest a lieutenant for cowardice the other day and threaten to have a sergeant shot for the same reason shortly afterwards. Were these officers, who all seemed to want to throw in the sponge, weak sisters, too? Or were they giving him the unvarnished truth? He needed someone he knew and trusted to give a real, honest assessment of the situation on the fortified goose-egg.

Then he remembered General Hoge of the 9th Armoured. He had known Bill Hoge since their days together at West Point. He knew 'what a calm, courageous, imperturbable fellow he was'. He knew too 'that nothing could ever flurry him and so above all I wanted to talk to him, to get his "feel" of the situation'.

He asked why Hoge wasn't at the conference. One of Clarke's staff said that he was still on his way to Commanster. Ridgway nodded, asked to be put in touch with him by radio and passed on the grid co-ordinates of a roadside farmhouse where the two generals could meet. Minutes later he was on his way.

Hoge arrived at the farmhouse at last light. Taking his old friend aside, out of earshot of any other officer present, a good indication of just how much Ridgway distrusted the 106th and 7th, he told Hoge:

'Bill, we've made contact now. This position is too exposed to try to hold it any longer.'

By now Ridgway knew that Montgomery had convinced Hodges to countermand Ridgway's order to defend the salient. The evacuation would have to go ahead; yet Ridgway was still unconvinced that an evacuation was necessary. Now everything depended on Hoge's reaction.

'We're not going to leave you in here,' Ridgway told him, 'to be chopped to pieces little by little. I'm going to extricate all the forces of the Seventh Armoured and attached units, including your own. I plan to start that withdrawal tonight. We're going to get you out of here.'

Hoge looked at his old friend. His green troops of the inexperienced 9th had done well, but they had paid the price. In one battalion alone there had been three commanders following each other in rapid succession. The men were at about the end of their tethers. They couldn't take any more. Finally he just said, 'How?'

That one word convinced Ridgway that the situation in the fortified goose-egg was as Hasbrouck's officers said it was—hopeless.

'Bill,' he said, 'we *can* and *will*.'

It is not known what was said during the rest of that conversation, but one might guess that Hoge told Ridgway a few home truths about what had really happened in St Vith during the last five days. We can assume this from Ridgway's next moves. Just before seven that night he reinstated Hasbrouck in command after suspending him earlier on, presumably because he felt the 7th Armoured commander was lacking in fighting spirit.

Then he stormed across to Jones's CP. Ridgway now realized that he had picked the wrong man for the overall command of the fortified goose-egg, and his bitterness comes out clearly in his own memoirs when he writes of Jones's CP that,

> It was many miles to the rear. The divisional commander was there. True, his division had been overrun and scattered and much of it was missing. But a good fraction of it was up there in that surrounded pocket fighting, and that's where he should have been.

At Jones's CP Ridgway ordered everyone out, save General Hasbrouck and his own deputy chief-of-staff, Colonel Quill. While the bewildered officers filed out, Ridgway stared at Jones grimly. His attitude seemed strange to the aggressive airborne commander. 'He appeared to be casual, almost indifferent, little interested in the fact that that night we were going to bring his people out of the trap.'

Naturally a man of Ridgway's temperament could not understand what had happened to Jones, a general who had seen his command disintegrate in a few short days. At that moment, behind that mask of indifference, a terrible turmoil must have been taking place in General Jones's heart. This was the moment of truth. Since his two regiments had vanished on the hills of the Snow Eifel he had forced himself to believe that he was in command, contributing something positive to the course of the war, lying to himself all the time. Now, staring at Ridgway's hard, unyielding face he knew the truth—he had been weighed in the balance and found wanting.

When the door had closed behind the last of the 106th officers, Ridgway turned to Colonel Quill and, to quote his own words, 'Quill at my direction wrote down in longhand my orders relieving this officer of his command.'

Then he turned to Hasbrouck, who now officially commanded the equivalent of two divisions, his own and the 106th, under its new chief General Perrin, and said, 'Bob, start pulling your people back as soon as possible. I want them all withdrawn under cover of darkness tonight.'*

While the 7th Armoured staff officers worked on their plans, passing on Montgomery's message from unit to unit—'They can come back with honour'—General Clarke's force began to withdraw. With only 100 tanks left and minus 4000 men, dead, captured and wounded, who had gone into battle at St Vith on 17 December, they withdrew in sullen glory.

At midnight on 22/23 December, Hasbrouck's plan to withdraw the 20,000 men in the fortified goose-egg was sent out to the front-line units in detail. A few minutes later a boxlike ambulance drew away from his CP in the direction of the city of Liège. It contained General Alan Jones. According to the best historian of the Battle of the Bulge, John Toland,† General Jones had fallen to the floor of the CP shortly after his interview with Ridgway because 'his heart—strained by worry, overwork, and tension—had

---

* In a more charitable version Colonel Dupuy, the 106th historian, says that Ridgway made Jones his assistant corps commander, and that Jones was left to work out the details of the withdrawal with Hasbrouck when he suffered his heart attack. I have accepted the Ridgway version.
† John Toland, *Battle: The Story of the Bulge.*

given way'. General Jones had suffered a serious heart attack, which would mean his retirement from the army.

Was that 'heart attack' a polite fiction to ease General Jones out of an impossible position? Was it a propaganda measure to cover up the failure in the American command at a black time in the Battle of the Bulge when many senior officers had failed and had lost their heads? Soon the many inquiries would start into the conduct of officers and units involved in the initial stages of the battle, but, at the moment, the corps of officers must present a united front to the world.* Or did General Jones, that sorely tried man, really suffer a heart attack? Perhaps it is not politic to inquire any further. For although General Jones was only one of many casualties, moral and physical, on the St Vith front during the Battle of the Bulge that December, there is something particularly tragic about his fate. A middle-aged man, he had spent the whole of his adult life in the US Army—a quarter of a century preparing for a war. Year in, year out, when the army had been thought of as a refuge for fools, reactionaries and work-shys, he had plodded through the hundred and one boring picayune tasks that make up the life of the peacetime soldier in some God-forsaken garrison town. He had sweated through the morning parades in the harsh sun of Texas, hiked through the choking dust of midwestern manoeuvres, faced the sullen, resentful eyes of two generations of young soldiers who had been 'gigged' for abusing an NCO or failing to salute the newest lieutenant on post, had listened to the same people making the same boring small talk in half a hundred similar officers' clubs. Year in, year out, to find out in one short week that it had all been for nothing, that he was a failure as a soldier. Within seven short days, he had seen a lifetime's work vanish as inexorably as he had seen his young division vanish, never to be replaced.†

Thus General Jones passes out of our picture, being driven slowly over the snowbound road that led to Liège, a casualty of the battle just as surely as if he had been struck by a bullet.

---

* After the battle, the inspector-general of the First Army, that most feared officer in any army, conducted investigations into the conduct of 106th Division, the 14th Cavalry Group, the 820th Tank Destroyer Battalion and the 106th Reconnaissance Troop—and that in the St Vith area alone.
† The 106th was reconstituted, but, apart from some local patrol action, its main task was to guard the massive concentrations of German PoWs on the Rhine.

Aftermath

'*Besser ein Ende mit Schrecken als ein Schrecken ohne Ende.*'*

German saying

A battle does not end when the echo of the last shot has vanished into the surrounding hills. Just as when a stone is thrown into a pond and the ripples spread outward, seemingly continuing for ever without cease, so it is with a great battle. For some it means tortured nightmares and waking bathed in sweat, fevered cries and commands of years before still echoing and re-echoing down the dark passages of the mind. For others it means bitter accusations and counter-accusations, the permanent souring of the personality. And for a few, the shooting and the suffering still goes on when the real battle is over.

As 1944 gave way to 1945, most of the officers of the 106th Division captured in the Snow Eifel, plus many of those of the 7th Division captured at St Vith, had been collected in *Oflag* VII.†
The officers' prisoner-of-war camp at Hammelburg was not a very inspiring sight. It lay on the top of the saucer-shaped plateau of a large hill, overlooking the little wine town of Hammelburg, where they have made wine since the time of Charlemagne, and out to the great windy artillery and rifle ranges, where German troops had trained for over fifty years.

The camp was divided into two compounds. The larger of the two housed 5000 Yugoslav officers, who had been there since 1941. But in spite of their four years behind barbed wire, the

---

* Better an end with horror than a horror without end.
† *Offizierslager*—officers' camp.

Yugoslavs were proud if shabby men, who were well organized and disciplined.

The smaller compound, a collection of low two-storey huts, made of wood and stone, housed some 1400 officers under the command of the senior US officer, Colonel Cavender. Most of the 106th officers among them were not a pleasant sight. They were scruffy, unkempt and ill-disciplined. And it was not only the food and the depression of prison life which made them so.*

The camp commandant, General von Goeckel, thought them 'unbelievably infantile' men who showed no respect for their own senior officers or the German ones. Unlike the Serbs they had not formed the usual prisoner 'collectives'; nor had they attempted to organize the normal prisoner entertainments—'language courses or camp theatres'. As far as the elderly German soldier knew 'they didn't even have an escape committee'.

What Goeckel didn't know was that these men's spirit had been broken. They had surrendered, many of them against their will and without their having fired a shot. Unkempt and dispirited, they lived for the high point of their day, the midday meal.

Thus the dreary months passed for the 106th men in *Oflag* VII and it seemed to them, cut off from news from home, that the war would never end. But, unknown to the shabby, starving men behind the barbed wire, the war was going to reach out and grab them in its grip one more time.

On the morning of 24 March 1945, General William Hoge, now commander of Patton's favourite division, the 4th Armoured, received a strange order from his corps commander, General Eddy.

'Bill,' the corps commander said over the phone, 'George [General Patton] wants a special expedition sent behind the lines to pick up nine hundred prisoners at Hammelburg.'

He filled Hoge in on the details and put down the phone, leaving Hoge wondering what was so special about the American

---

* Colonel Joe Matthews, former executive officer of the 422nd, recalls that their staple diet was 'green hornet soup', made of beet tops and horsemeat. It got its name because its surface was covered with maggots stained green from the beets. Among the 'kriegies', there was often heated discussion whether the maggots should be eaten or not. Matthews, an ex-agricultural chemist, decided they were protein and ate them.

PoWs that made Patton suggest a harebrained raid sixty miles behind the German lines to rescue them.

Two days later, on the 26th, the immaculately uniformed Third Army commander himself turned up at General Eddy's HQ. He was met by Brigadier-General Canine, Eddy's chief-of-staff. Patton snapped: 'Pick up the phone and get Bill Hoge. And tell him to cross the Main River and get to Hammelburg!'

Canine told Patton what General Eddy had insisted he say if the army commander made an appearance at the corps HQ: 'General, the last thing Matt told me before he left was that if you came by and told us to issue that order, I was to tell you I wasn't to do it.'

Canine waited for the storm to descend upon him. Patton was well known in the Third Army for the sharpness of his tongue. But, surprisingly enough, Patton remained calm. He said softly, 'Get Hoge on the phone and I'll tell him myself.'

Quickly Patton explained to Hoge what he wanted from the 4th Armoured. Hoge protested that he couldn't spare a man or a vehicle for such a harebrained scheme. Still Patton didn't lose his temper. Indeed his high-pitched voice took on a wheedling tone which surprised and shocked Hoge.

'Bill,' Patton said, 'I promise I'll replace every man and every vehicle you lose. . . . I promise!'

Putting down the phone, the completely bewildered Hoge looked across the room at Major Al Stiller, Patton's senior aide who was at his divisional HQ, and asked what the hell was so important about Hammelburg PoW Camp. The leathery-faced, ex-Texas Ranger explained. The Old Man wanted Hammelburg liberated because his own son-in-law, Colonel John Waters, was a prisoner-of-war there!

On the afternoon of 26 March 1945, Colonel Abrams, one day to be an army commander like the man he had succeeded as commander of the 4th Armoured's CCB, Bruce Clarke, ordered Captain Abe Baum, a former pattern cutter in a Bronx ladies' blouse factory, to break through to Hammelburg and rescue the prisoners. Abrams ended with the statement: 'The division is not to follow you—you'll be on your own. We'll give you the best we have available. You're to get back to us whichever way you can.'

After Baum had gone, Abrams snapped at Stiller, 'If this mission is accomplished that guy deserves a Congressional Medal of Honor!'

But the mission was *not* accomplished. Amazingly enough Baum managed to make his way, with his 300-man force, through the lines of a whole German division, and over the next forty-eight hours thrust sixty miles deep into German territory. He broke into the prison camp and liberated the men of 106th and 7th Armoured, though Patton's son-in-law, Waters, for whom it had all been staged, was seriously wounded during the liberation.

But then tragedy struck and the ill-fated 106th's luck ran out once again. An SS battalion attacked Baum's exhausted force. Major Boyer, who had guided the 7th Armoured to St Vith, was taken once again while manning a machine-gun. Lieutenant Alan Jones Jr was recaptured while trying to hobble away on his frostbitten feet. Baum was also wounded and captured.

Three men managed to get back from the raid, struggling into the US lines two days later—three men out of the 300 who had set out, plus an unknown number of prisoners who had set out on the return journey.* The unlucky 106th men were fated to spend another two terrible months behind barbed wire, losing more and more men to Allied air attacks.

Finally it was over. In the Ardennes the local authorities dared to venture into the woods once more. Swiftly they planted quick-growing firs around the scenes of death and destruction, hoping that they would hide the ugly scars of war.

In Washington, the Pentagon attempted to do the same, trying to conceal what had happened with official whitewash, just as General Patton tried to hide the real reason for the ill-fated Hammelburg Raid. The events at St Vith, which were associated with the scandalous conduct of the 106th Division (although Clarke's brave defence of the key road and rail centre did as much to de-

---

* General von Goeckel estimates that he had 100 *more* prisoners in the camp *after* the raid. Some 150-200 men were unaccounted for. That was the cost of Patton's plan.

feat the German offensive as any other action in that great battle),
had to be played down. Bastogne, the victory, had to be played
up. General MacAuliffe's celebrated 'Nuts' reply to the German
demand for the surrender of the town went into the history books
and became part of American patriotic lore.

But there were vital lessons to be learned from the 106th's be-
haviour in the Snow Eifel, which the Pentagon refused to learn—to
its cost.

General Bruce Clarke laid it on the line when he wrote in the
School of Armor's official study of the St Vith battle:

> In this type of defensive action, leadership, even though more
> difficult than in other situations, is a primary prerequisite. When
> men are faced by odds which seem overwhelming, and other units
> are pulling out to the rear, only the highest type of leadership will
> prevail. To regroup men who have once been overrun by the enemy
> and to make another stand against the same enemy is a challenge of
> the utmost proportions to the leadership of any unit!

What was wrong with the leadership of the 106th Division and
the 14th Cavalry? We have seen that General Jones, Colonels
Devine, Cavender and Descheneaux all failed as leaders with tragic
results for their men.

Why did they fail? I think that James Jones, an infantryman in
the pre-war US Regular Army, has explained better than any professional military author in his *Graphic Art of WWII* what went
wrong. He writes:

> It was probably simple vanity and pride which made Eisenhower,
> Marshall and company believe untested US soldiers could go head-
> long straight on into the France of Hitler's 'Fortress Europe' and
> win. The US officer corps of those days before the war lived in a
> sort of sealed-off plastic shell of their own making which could sup-
> port such unrealistic dreams. The Great Depression years hurt them
> less than most citizens. Low-salaried though they were, their crea-
> ture comforts were well seen to, by even lower-salaried enlisted
> slaves; and they could live well on their well-gardened, manicured
> posts and forts with booze and food at PX prices, and conduct their
> obsolete little training exercises with the same flair that they used to
> conduct the Saturday night officers' club dances. . . . But they were
> brave men and dedicated, and intelligent, great men a few of them,

and with a Churchill and a Roosevelt to guide them, and some time in the field in a war to humble them a little, they could and would do great things to preserve the nation.

But the senior officers of the 106th Division did not have that 'time in the field in a war to humble them a little'. The division was caught completely unprepared for action. Its staff proved itself slow, inefficient and lacking in aggressiveness. Right from top to bottom, the staff officers were paralysed by the fact that *they* were actually being attacked; that the Germans were coming for *them;* that the bullets were intended to kill *them.*

So what did they do? They did the worst of all things when under attack—nothing. Colonel Descheneaux and Colonel Cavender and their superior, Jones, simply failed to react to the all-out German assault on the two regiments' flanks.

But the fault lay deeper than just inertia on the part of the officers. As Eisenhower wrote in his own account of that campaign, *Crusade in Europe:*

> At the war's beginning the average Army officer, both regular and civilian, placed too much faith in surface discipline, based solely upon perfection in the mechanics of training. Commanders are habitually diffident where they are called to deal with subjects that touch the human soul—aspirations, ideals, inner beliefs, affection, hatreds. No matter how earnestly commanders may attempt to influence a soldier's habits, his training, his conduct or extol the virtues of gallantry and fortitude, they shyly stop short of going into matters which they fear may be interpreted as preaching.

There was no 'Crusade in Europe' for the young soldiers of the 106th Infantry Division. We have seen how they told their German captors that they didn't know why they were 'over here' and that they had it 'much better at home'. They had not been prepared by their leaders for what was to come, and they had no inner pride—what the military call *'esprit de corps'*—in themselves or their outfit, not to speak of their country, which would fortify them and allow them to face up to the challenge when it came.

An outfit's morale is based on practical considerations such as weapons, food, the terrain in which they must fight and factors such as the state of the weather and the deterioration of their efficiency due to time in combat and the resultant exhaustion. To that one can add other items like their home backgrounds, the kind of training they had received, the strength of the friendships they have made with their fellow soldiers. But the basis of all this complicated amalgam is confidence in leadership, confidence that the officers who command you in battle know what they are doing. Lacking this leadership, even the best-equipped troops—and American troops have always been the most generously and best-equipped soldiers in all the wars fought in the twentieth century—will crumple when hit hard.

The defeat of the 106th Infantry Division in the Snow Eifel was the first break in that easy optimistic confidence with which America's military leaders, now finally out of Jones's 'sealed-off plastic shell', approached the affairs of the world outside America. They believed that if one knew the facts, had the necessary equipment, used the good old American know-how and 'get up and go', one could master any situation. In the Snow Eifel, that attitude was proved wrong for the first of many times in the years to come. In December 1944, the US Army had all the things mentioned above, yet its leaders had overlooked one, *the human factor*. And the Pentagon would keep overlooking that human factor, confident that the military machine could not be stopped by such a minor and intangible factor until that general who had once sent Baum to break into Hammelburg Camp finally had to concede to defeat on the other side of the world.*

Long after Abrams, Jones and Cavender were dead and Hoge and Clarke retired, the battle of the Snow Eifel claimed one last victim —Colonel Jochen Peiper of the 1st SS Panzer Division, 'the Adolf Hitler Bodyguard', whose Tigers had broken through the eastern route of the 7th Armoured's race for St Vith.

Accused of the murder of US prisoners at Malmédy, just above the spot where the 7th Armoured's chief-of-staff, Colonel Church Matthews was ambushed, he was sentenced to death by a US court

---

* It is interesting to note that General Clarke, now a four-star general, was called out of retirement by the president to investigate the situation in Vietnam and came back to report what he had always reported when questioned about morale—improved leadership was needed.

in 1946.* His sentence was commuted to life and in 1957 he was finally released from jail. Thereafter he moved from job to job. But his past always caught up with him in the end and he was forced to move on. In 1969, in a last interview with this author, he said, 'I'm sitting on a powder keg. Ellis, Kempner and Wiesenthal†—they have all tried to get me in the past. Someone will come along one day with another "story" and the powder keg will explode under me. Then it'll be all over at last.'

Thereafter the ex-SS colonel left Germany for good and went to live in France so that he could 'find peace at last'. There he built himself a small house in a wood and set about earning a living by translating military books from English into German.

Peiper lived in peace in his self-imposed French exile for eight years, avoiding too much contact with the locals, concentrating simply on earning a living. But this peace came to an end abruptly on 21 June 1976. At the entrance to Traves that morning, the surprised villagers found a large swastika, the SS runes and the name Peiper painted on the road. That day a van load of communists came to the village and started distributing pamphlets calling on the astonished villagers to demonstrate against Peiper.

On the following morning Peiper went to the police. There he was told the local Prefect was under 'increasing pressure from Paris . . . to expel him from France'. Peiper was now forced to receive journalists and photographers every day who wanted to know more about his 'criminal past'. As he wrote to a friend, 'The atmosphere is as if they have discovered me in my hiding place after a long hunt. My peaceful paradise has become a besieged position, but I will hold this position to the bitter end.'

In the first week of July, Peiper received his final warning. It read: 'We've told you often enough—take off! But you're still there. Now you've only yourself to thank for what is going to happen to you.' The note, naturally, was unsigned.

Peiper decided to stay on. As a security measure he sent his

---

* See C. Whiting, *Massacre at Malmédy*, Leo Cooper, 1972, for further details.
† Colonel Ellis was the man who prosecuted him at his trial. Dr Kempner was one of the prosecutors at the Nuremberg trial. Herr Wiesenthal is the man who found Eichmann.

wife and daughter, Kathie, back to Germany, and wrote a plea for help to the German embassy in Paris. In it he stated:

It is true that I was a colonel in the SS and that in my younger days I was posted to Himmler as his military adjutant. It is also true that the Americans sentenced me and many of my comrades-in-arms to death at the notorious Malmédy Trial of 1946. But in the Federal Republic of Germany I am regarded as a citizen without a criminal record and here in France I haven't done anything wrong either. Therefore, I beg you to give me legal protection.

But by the time the German ambassador, Sigismund von Braun (brother of Werner, the missile expert), received the letter it was already too late.

On 14 July 1976 all of France was celebrating the 187th anniversary of the storming of the Bastille. In Traves, the sixty-three people who made up the community had already finished their celebrations and had retired to bed, when at midnight shots disturbed the silence. For a while the locals took them for some drunken farmer setting off fireworks, ending the day's holiday in one last noisy outburst. But when the 'fireworks' persisted and someone saw the flames rising into the sky from the direction of the wood where Peiper's house was located, the fire brigade was alerted. The voluntary firemen tumbled out of their beds and ran, half-dressed, to their engine. They were in for an unpleasant surprise. In the shed they found their hoses had been slashed and made useless. Now the villagers realized that something strange was happening. Finally, after some debate, the police were called.

They arrived at dawn. But it was already too late. Jochen Peiper's wooden house was burned to the ground. Poking through the smoking ruins, they came upon a horrible sight. A pitch-black lump of charred flesh, less than two feet in length, with next to it a Colt, Smith & Wesson hunting rifle, its magazine empty. They had found what was left of Peiper. He had died, fighting off the attack of a group known as the 'Avengers', who telephoned the Paris newspaper *L'Aurore* next day and claimed credit for his death. When they had been unable to overcome his resistance with their weapons, they had thrown a number of petrol bombs at the wooden structure of his Bavarian-style chalet and set it on fire, burning him to death.

The ripples which had started in Lanzerath's Café Palm so long before when Peiper had finally broken through the Gap and opened the way for the final encirclement of the 422nd and 423rd had come to rest at last.

Bibliography

O. Bradley. *A Soldier's Story*. London: Eyre & Spottiswoode, 1951

H. Cole. *Battle of the Bulge*. Washington: Office of the Chief of Military History, 1965

M. Delaval. *La Bataille des Ardennes*. Brussels: Imprimerie Médicale, 1958

R. E. Dupuy. 'Lion in the way', *Infantry Journal*. New York, 1949

D. Eisenhower. *Crusade in Europe*. New York: Doubleday, 1948

J. Eisenhower. *The Bitter Woods*. New York: Putnam 1969 & Nicolson, 1967

P. Elstob. *Hitler's Last Offensive*. New York: Macmillan 19–

K. Fagnoul. *Kriegsschicksale*. Geschichtsverein Venn-Eifel. St Vith, Belgium, 1971

C. MacDonald. *Company Commander*. New York: Ballantine, 1947

R. Merriam. *Dark December*. London: Ziff Davies, 1947

B. Montgomery. *Normandy to the Baltic*. London: Hutchinson, 1947

J. Nobecourt. *Hitler's Last Gamble*. New York: Schocken

M. Ridgway. *Soldier: The Memoirs of Matthew B. Ridgway*. New York: Harper & Row, 1956

P. Schramm. *Kriegstagebuch der OKW*. Munich: Bernard & Graefe, 1961

M. Shulman. *Defeat in the West*. New York: E. P. Dutton, 1954

M. Shulman, ed. *The Battle of St Vith, Belgium*. Washington: The US Armor School, 1950

J. Toland. *Battle: The Story of the Bulge*. New York: Random House, 1959

H. von Manteuffel. *The Battle of the Ardennes*. London: André Deutsch, 1965

C. Wagener. 'Strittige Fragen zur Ardennenoffensive', Wehrwissenschaftliche Rundschau. Stuttgart, 1961

W. Warlioment. *Inside Hitler's Headquarters: 1939-45*. London: Weidenfeld & Nicolson, 1946

C. Whiting. *Bloody Aachen*. New York: Stein and Day, 1976

Decision at St Vith. New York: Ballantine, 1969

Massacre at Malmédy. New York: Stein and Day, 1971

Skorzeny. New York: Ballantine, 1972

Index